Catch-22

Antiheroic Antinovel

TWAYNE'S MASTERWORK STUDIES
ROBERT LECKER, GENERAL EDITOR

.

Catch-22

Antiheroic Antinovel

STEPHEN W. POTTS

TWAYNE PUBLISHERS • BOSTON
A Division of G. K. Hall & Co.

PS
3515
.E33
C3385
1989

Twayne's Masterwork Studies No. 29

Published by Twayne Publishers
A division of G. K. Hall & Co.
70 Lincoln Street, Boston, Massachusetts 02111

Copyediting supervised by Barbara Sutton.
Book production by Janet Z. Reynolds.
Typeset in 10/14 Sabon
by Compset, Inc., of Beverly, Massachusetts.

Printed on permanent/durable acid-free paper
and bound in the United States of America.

Library of Congress Cataloging-in-Publication Data

Potts, Stephen W., 1949-
Catch-22 : antiheroic antinovel / Stephen W. Potts.
p.   cm.—(Twayne's masterwork studies ; no. 29)
Bibliography: p.
Includes index.
ISBN 0-8057-7992-2 (alk. paper).
ISBN 0-8057-8041-6 (pbk. : alk. paper)
1. Heller, Joseph.   Catch-22.   I. Title.   II. Series.
PS3558.E476C3385   1989
813'.54—dc19

88-33277
CIP

Contents

Note on the References
and Acknowledgments

For this study I have used the standard Dell pocketbook edition of *Catch-22*. All parenthetical page references are keyed to that edition.

I wish to thank Marcella Berger, vice president and director of subsidiary rights in the Trade Division of Simon & Schuster, for her permission to use the photograph of Joseph Heller from the jacket of the original (1961) hardcover edition of *Catch-22*. And I would like to thank Joseph Heller himself for his transcontinental telephone call directing me to Ms. Berger on this matter. For the record, his personal assistance was well worth my exiting a Saturday morning shower to answer the phone.

Joseph Heller, 1961
Photograph courtesy of Simon & Schuster

Chronology:
Joseph Heller's Life and Works

1923	Joseph Heller born 1 May in the Coney Island section of Brooklyn, New York, the youngest of three. His parents are first-generation Jewish immigrants; his father, Isaac Heller, arrived from Russia in 1913, and his mother, Lena, never learned English well. Isaac, a socialist and agnostic, drives a bakery delivery truck.
1929	Isaac Heller dies following an operation. Joseph begins his education at Coney Island's Public School No. 188. During his school career he will form his most enduring friendships, including one with George Mandel, also destined to become a writer.
1941	Graduates from Abraham Lincoln High School. Works as a file clerk in an insurance office. With America's entry into World War II, becomes a blacksmith's helper in Norfolk Navy Yard.
1942	Joins Army as a Shipping File Clerk. In October, enlists in U.S. Army Air Corps. Having heard that the average life span of a gunner in combat is three days, enrolls in cadet school.
1944	Graduates from cadet school as 1st lieutenant and bombardier and is stationed in Corsica with the 488th Squadron of the Twelfth Air Force. Flies sixty missions over the Mediterranean as a wing bombardier. Upon his honorable discharge receives an Air Medal and a Presidential Unit Citation.
1945	Marries Shirley Held. Enrolls on the GI Bill at the University of Southern California. Publishes his first short story, "I Don't Love You Any More," in an issue of *Story* magazine (September/October) devoted to the fiction of returning veterans.
1946	Transfers to New York University.
1947	Attends a creative writing course taught by Maurice Baudin

and grows convinced of his aptitude for fiction. Writes a handful of short stories he will publish over the succeeding years.

1948   Receives B.A. and a Phi Beta Kappa. Publishes "Castle of Snow" and "A Man Named Flute" in *Atlantic Monthly*, "Girl from Greenwich" and "Nothing To Be Done" in *Esquire*.

1949   Earns M.A. in American Literature at Columbia University with thesis on "The Pulitzer Plays: 1917–1935." Heads for Oxford University in England on a Fulbright scholarship.

1950   Returns to the U.S. to teach composition at Pennsylvania State University.

1952   Leaves academe to take a job as advertising manager at *Time* magazine.

1955   Still working for *Time*, he begins to put together the materials for a novel loosely based on his war experiences, entitled *Catch-18*. The first tentative chapter appears as a short story of that name in the anthology *New World Writing No. 7*.

1956   Leaves *Time* for another position as advertising manager at *Look* magazine.

1958   Takes a job as promotion manager at *McCall's*. Signs a contract with Simon and Schuster for his war novel. Its title will be changed to *Catch-22* to avoid confusion with Leon Uris's *Mila-18*.

1959   His story "McAdam's Log" appears in *Gentleman's Quarterly*.

1961   *Catch-22* published. Heller returns to academe to teach fiction and dramatic writing at Yale and the University of Pennsylvania.

1963   His undergraduate story "World Full of Great Cities" published in *Nelson Algren's Book of Lonesome Monsters*.

1964   Turns to full-time writing, completing a screenplay for the Warner Brothers film *Sex and the Single Girl* and helping with the pilot for the television show "McHale's Navy" under the pseudonym Max Orange. Soon afterward begins work on *Something Happened*.

1967   Interrupts work on *Something Happened* to polish script of film *Casino Royale* (working on some scenes also revised by Woody Allen) and to write the play *We Bombed in New Haven*.

1968   *We Bombed in New Haven* performed at Yale and on Broadway for eighty-six performances between October and December before closing to mixed reviews. Heller returns to *Something Happened*.

1970 Interrupts novel again to polish script of *Dirty Dingus Magee* and write *Catch-22: A Dramatization.* Mike Nichols's movie of *Catch-22* appears, drawing readers back to book and sending it for the first time onto American best-seller lists.

1971 *Catch-22: A Dramatization* opens for two-week engagement in East Hampton, New York. Heller returns to the teaching of literature, fiction writing, and dramatic writing at City College of New York.

1973 Samuel French publishes Heller's one-act play *Clevinger's Trial.*

1974 *Something Happened* published; reviews mixed, but novel is immediate best-seller. Income from his two novels reaches $1.25 million.

1975 Leaves his teaching job at CCNY. As the Watergate scandal and then the Vietnam War draw to a close, he begins work on *Good as Gold.*

1979 Publication of *Good as Gold.*

1980 Begins work on *God Knows.*

1981 Separates from wife Shirley. In December he suffers a sudden attack of paralysis. Admitted to Mount Sinai Hospital, he learns he has Guillain-Barré syndrome, a rare form of polyneuritis.

1982 During rehabilitative therapy he begins an affair with nurse Valerie Humphries. Released from medical care in summer.

1984 Publication of *God Knows.* Divorce final after a long court battle and $270,000 in legal costs.

1986 Publication of *No Laughing Matter.* Co-authored with friend Speed Vogel, it tells of Heller's ordeal with Guillain-Barré.

1987 Marries Valerie Humphries in April. Resumes teaching at the University of Pennsylvania while finishing *Picture This,* a novel focusing on Rembrandt's Holland and Aristotle's Athens.

1988 Publication of *Picture This.*

I

Historical Context

At twenty-one years of age, Lieutenant Joseph Heller was enjoying World War II. As a bombardier stationed in Corsica, he joined his fellow airmen in splitting time between fighting the forces of fascism from their ponderous planes and playing baseball and basketball. Following the liberation of Rome in June 1944, he often visited the apartments leased there by his group's efficient executive officer. With companions like Joe Chrenko, who on one such excursion pretended to be a photographer from *Life* magazine, Lieutenant Heller sampled Roman wine and women, with some song undoubtedly thrown in to make the experience complete.

On his thirty-seventh mission, a bombing run over Avignon in southern France, the co-pilot of his B-25, fearing the bomber was about to stall, grabbed the controls in panic and sent the plane into a steep dive. Heller found himself pressed against the ceiling of his compartment in the bomber's nose with his headset torn loose, unable to communicate with anyone for several terrible seconds. When the plane leveled off and he was able to plug back into the intercom, he heard the sobbing voice of the co-pilot: "Help him! Help him!" "Help who?" asked Lieutenant Heller. "Help the bombardier," came the reply. Heller experienced a deathly chill. "*I'm* the bombardier," he replied at last. "I'm all right."

When he crawled into the rear of the plane, however, he did find a casualty, a young gunner with a wound in the thigh. Heller treated him with first aid, and the entire crew returned alive to the base. That was the young lieutenant's closest brush with death during the war. And although he dutifully flew another twenty-three combat missions, the war was not as much fun after Avignon.

When Heller and the other men of his generation came home after defeating Hitler and Tojo, they returned to a United States ebullient with power and optimism. After a decade and a half of depression and armed conflict, America was back—the only nation in the world that was better off after the war than before it.

Some members of Heller's generation soon produced novels about the war, of which the most celebrated were probably Norman Mailer's *The Naked and the Dead* and James Jones's *From Here to Eternity.* These were grittily realistic, tough-minded books reminiscent of Ernest Hemingway's handling of earlier wars. Ex-lieutenant Heller also turned his hand to writing; as a college student on the GI Bill he, too, worked in the modernist mode of realism, though he avoided war topics. Instead he began, as he later told *Playboy* interviewer Sam Merrill, as a writer of *New Yorker* stories about "Jewish families in the Depression," or as an author in the *Esquire* style of Hemingway, Irwin Shaw, and John O'Hara.[1]

He imitated his models well enough to have his undergraduate pieces published not only in *Esquire*, but also in the *Atlantic Monthly* and other magazines of the literary establishment. His first *Atlantic* story, "Castle of Snow," is about a Jewish family in the depression; his second, "A Man Named Flute," in its glance at big-city gangster life suggests the fiction of *Esquire* regular Nelson Algren by way of Hemingway's "The Killers." Even more typical of the *Esquire* style of sordid naturalism is Heller's undergraduate story "World Full of Great Cities," published in Nelson Algren's 1963 anthology *Book of Lonesome Monsters.* In this vignette a delivery boy fulfills an errand to a New York flat and finds himself the target of a half-hearted attempt at seduction by a man and a woman. When the woman backs out, the boy leaves intact, albeit confused and vaguely ill. By the time he graduated, however, Joseph Heller had given up wanting to write such imitative modernist tales.

Heller left college as America entered the fifties. Once again the business of America was business, and business was booming—not least in the military-industrial complex, whose business was bombing. Having learned an important lesson from the economic fallout of World War II, the United States geared up for the cold war, which was fought overseas in Korea and Berlin and at home in Hollywood, the State Department, the halls of academe, and anywhere else Senator Joseph McCarthy and the forces of the Right suspected the presence of the Left. It was a time of red-baiting and blacklisting, while the public palliated the fact of the ever-growing ever-presence of The Bomb by tuning in to that other great technological marvel of the era, television. General Eisenhower was in the White House, and former General Motors president Charles E. Wilson, his Secretary of Defense, could announce that was was good for GM was good for the country.

Amid this milieu in 1953, Joseph Heller began work on his first novel. Though he had traded a career in teaching English for a series of advertising posts with popular magazines, he had pursued his interest in literature on his own. His reading ranged from the classic nineteenth-century novelists Dickens and Dostoyevski to modernist William Faulkner, modern absurdist Nathanael West, and early postmodernist Vladimir Nabokov. Around the time of reading Nabokov's blackly humorous *Laughter in the Dark* he discovered the avant-garde French writer Louis-Ferdinand Céline, whose career had begun in 1932 with his savage masterpiece *Journey to the End of the Night.* Heller was much impressed.

Céline's book is rooted in World War I, though its attitude toward war is wholly different from the modernist's Hemingwayesque attitude of heroic endurance in the face of the tragic ironies of life. Céline's hero, Ferdinand Bardamu, meets irony with irony, and the wartime world with obscenity, cowardice, and indifference to any issues but his own survival, and finally with madness. He greets grotesque images of death with equally grotesque contempt, as when he observes that a cavalryman killed by a shell "hadn't his head anymore, only his neck open at the top with blood bubbling in it like stew in a pot."[2] Bardamu has nothing against the Germans, but much to detest in the officers and other authorities who have laid his life on the front line. For Céline's picaresque protagonist, life is all "Lie, copulate, and die."[3]

In structure the novel jumps from scene to scene through time and space, more or less chronologically, but with little hint of how much time has passed from one episode to the next. Heller noted that "Céline did things with time and structure and colloquial speech I'd never experienced before" and claimed that *Journey to the End of the Night* was the book that touched . . . off" the conception of *Catch-22*.[4] Once the writing of the novel began, however, Heller brought in elements from across the spectrum of his reading, from the classics to the modernists to the absurdists, with a good dose of popular humor and contemporary satire tossed in.

When the first published excerpt of the novel, "Catch-18," appeared in *New Worlds Writing* 7 in 1955, it reflected mostly the latter influence, resembling little more than a wacky look at the military reminiscent of Max Shulman, Sergeant Bilko, and *No Time for Sergeants,* lacking even the serious undertone of wartime comedies like *Mr. Roberts* and *Stalag 17.* But when the full novel appeared in 1961, readers soon discovered that it was something different.

2

The Importance of the Work

By the end of the decade of the fifties, with its smug, even soporific conservatism, American intellectual culture was restless. Historian Arthur Schlesinger, Jr., expressed the discontent of his fellow intellectuals in an article in the January 1960 *Esquire*. After insisting that a new desire for change was rumbling beneath the "passivity and acquiescence" of the Eisenhower epoch, he goes on to say:

> As yet, the feeling is inchoate and elusive. But it is beginning to manifest itself in a multitude of ways: in freshening attitudes in politics; in a new acerbity in criticism; in stirrings, often tinged with desperation, among the youth; in a spreading contempt everywhere for reigning clichés. There is evident a widening restlessness, dangerous tendencies toward satire and idealism, a mounting dissatisfaction with the official priorities, a deepening concern with our character and objectives as a nation.[5]

Among the examples he gives of this cultural foment are the rise of the Beats, the sudden efflorescence of satire and "sick humor," and the popularity of books critical of American culture and capitalism, such as Galbraith's *The Affluent Society*, Riesman's *The Lonely Crowd*, and Whyte's *The Organization Man*.

In American literary circles many critics were seeking an alternative for the mainstream mimetic novel, which had been pronounced dead by a number of them following the great prewar era that had produced the masterpieces of the modernist canon. For many, James Joyce's *Ulysses* and *Finnegans Wake* had taken the realistic novel as far as it could go, even to the brink of mythic fantasy. Many looked for guidance to Europe, and France in particular, where they found the existentialist novels of Camus and Sartre, the Theater of the Absurd, and the *nouvelle roman* of Alain Robbe-Grillet. None translated well to the needs of American fiction, however.

Other possibilities were suggested by the fiction of Vladimir Nabokov and Argentinian Jorge Luis Borges. As later noted by English critic Tony Tanner in his 1971 study *City of Words*, Nabokov and Borges took up the challenge left by Joyce.[6] Both had begun in the realistic tradition that the twentieth century inherited from the nineteenth, but steered into newer realms of invention with the examples of Joyce and Kafka in their back pockets. Both authors offered the further advantage, for Americans, of being alienated from their own cultures and thus cosmopolitan in outlook—Nabokov was the scion of an aristocratic Russian family transplanted to central Europe and then America, Borges received the whole of his education in Europe—and for both English was a second language. Both had caught the attention of the American literary intelligentsia in the 1950s, Borges with his collection *Fictions*, Nabokov with *Lolita*; both works had been first published and celebrated in France.

Amid the literary ferment of letters after Joyce, amid the restlessness and satire and general questioning of American political and artistic values, the new decade of the sixties began. Arthur Schlesinger, Jr., predicted that it would be "spirited, articulate, inventive, incoherent, turbulent, with energy shooting off wildly in all directions."[7]

Into this environment in the first year of the Kennedy presidency came *Catch-22*. As the blurb inside the book jacket of the first hardcover edition notes, "CATCH-22 is like no other novel we have ever read. It has its own style, its own rationale, its own extraordinary character. It moves back and forth from hilarity to horror. It is outrageously funny and strangely affecting. It is totally original." Many reviewers agreed. They recognized the novel's links with war humor and black humor, but the blend of farce, fierce violence, sharp satire, and the avant-garde method of the plot set *Catch-22* apart.

In fact, *Catch-22* was the first of a slew of novels in the early sixties that represented a new direction in American literature, combining naturalistic detail with satirical and surreal exaggeration, mingling slapstick and gloom, fantasy and history, real issues and two-dimensional caricatures that are at best reminiscent of Charles Dickens. Other works of this groundbreaking moment are Ken Kesey's *One Flew Over the Cuckoo's Nest* (1962), Kurt Vonnegut's *Mother Night* (1961) and *Cat's Cradle* (1963), and Thomas Pynchon's *V* (1963). Not until the 1970s would American critics recognize that these novels were not aberrations fitting loosely within the black humor genre, but the advance guard of a whole new approach to the novel, a movement now generally given the term "postmodernism."

But postmodernism was not even a glimmer in the critic's eye when *Catch-22* reached the British best-seller lists in its first year. And the novel's American readership was probably hooked as much on the book's message as on its method. In this Heller was helped along by national events. By the middle of the decade the "police action" in Vietnam was heating up to a full-scale war under President Johnson, and both progressive intellectuals and college students began to show an increasing annoyance with the liberal regime that had come in with the late JFK. By 1965 Berkeley's Free Speech movement had caught the attention of other campus activists, and increasingly the idealism that had earlier been channeled into civil rights and the Peace Corps began to mobilize against the growing war and America's cold war foreign policy in general, and from there against every aspect of American life as represented by "the Establishment."

Where the more sullen, quietly rebellious college students of the 1950s had embraced J. D. Salinger and Jack Kerouac, the activist readers of the 1960s—having graduated from the satirical if sophomoric sick humor of *Mad* magazine to the sterner leftist critiques of Herbert Marcuse and Paul Goodman—found their confirmation in the pointed social satires of Heller, Vonnegut, and Kesey. Of all the innovative books of radical style and social criticism, *Catch-22* is probably the most encyclopedic in the number of issues it touches on; in so completely capturing the frustration of the individual up against powerful and faceless bureaucracies, it gave the American language a new term in "Catch-22," which has come to refer to any situation encompassing paradoxical choices, usually imposed from above.

Heller could honestly claim that his novel was not intended as a criticism of World War II, or initially even of war in general; that its satire was aimed at the cold war of the fifties is clear, he observed in interviews, from the pointed use of anachronisms such as loyalty oaths, helicopters, and IBM machines.[8] Nonetheless, in the eyes of the youth of the time Heller and his novel were most identified with the antiwar issue, an identification he encouraged with his 1969 antiwar play *We Bombed in New Haven*. When, at the end of the decade, the novel was filmed by Mike Nichols (long a satirist in his own right), it joined a string of darkly humorous antiwar films with a youthful cult following: *Dr. Strangelove, How I Won the War* (featuring John Lennon), and *M*A*S*H*.

With the coming of the seventies campus activism faded away, as eventually, and ignominiously, did the war itself and the presidents who conducted it. But as *Catch-22* moved from backpack to assigned reading list the stature of the novel remained secure. As one of the first and most original creations of literary postmodernism and as an artifact of the social and political culture of the sixties, it is still regarded by many as the best novel of the decade.

3

Critical Reception

When *Catch-22* appeared in October 1961, there was no such consensus on its merits. One of the first compliments it received in print came from an interview with humorist S. J. Perelman in the *New York Herald Tribune*; when asked if he had read any good books lately, he answered, "*Catch-22*," no doubt recognizing the affinity of its surreal comedy with his own. In one of the most positive of the formal reviews, Nelson Algren, in *The Nation*, ended with the assertion that *Catch-22* was "not merely the best American novel to come out of World War II; it is the best American novel that has come out of anywhere in years."[9] He particularly praised the book for its repudiation of the malevolent hypocrisies of American civilization. Robert Brustein, writing for the similarly progressive periodical the *New Republic*, recommended it on like grounds and recognized its technical and comic affinities to the Marx Brothers, Max Shulman, and S. J. Perelman, along with a "mordant intelligence, closer to that of Nathanael West."[10] In general, these critics and others who liked the book noted its zany humor, its pointed satire, its avant-garde stylistic complexity, and its grotesque horrors. Some compared it to past classics of satire by Voltaire, Swift, and Samuel Butler.

These positive views were nearly balanced, however, by those reviewers who saw the novel as offensive, unpatriotic, vulgar, and incoherent. Many, even some who praised the book, thought it excessive—in length and redundancy, in comic effects, in the graphic depiction of sex and gore; such remarks appeared in the *New Yorker,* the *New York Times,* and the *New York Herald Tribune.* The harshest review came in late from the anonymous pen of Roger H. Smith in *Daedalus;* he extensively criticized *Catch-22* for an immoral philosophy, artless writing, and unbelievable characters and plot, concluding that the whole effort was "worthless."[11]

A number of issues recurred in these reviews, pointing the way for the more analytical critics to follow. For the most part, these issues revolved around either Heller's technique or his message. In the first category stood the matter of the novel's tortured chronology, its broad comedy and its characters, and its style. In the latter lay discussions of Heller's satirical targets and his themes. Perhaps the most frequent complaint made by supporters and detractors alike bridged both categories: it addressed the sudden twist in the last part of the novel, where the plot becomes more or less chronological, the tone more serious, and Yossarian less of a picaresque caricature as he wrestles with his conscience over the decision to desert. In large part these early reviews have defined the parameters of subsequent criticism.

Despite the contempt of some reviewers and the doubts of others, *Catch-22* did not go away. After becoming an instant best-seller in England and an underground favorite with the college crowd in a decade of increasing social criticism, the novel spawned a number of essays dealing with the objects of its satire. Among the first was Frederick R. Karl's 1964 article "Joseph Heller's *Catch-22:* Only Fools Walk in Darkness," which proposes that the novel dramatizes the full absurdity of all modern life, that Yossarian undertakes a sort of existential quest in pursuit of freedom, sanity, and a sensual confirmation of the flesh.[12] Likewise, Norman Podhoretz, in his chapter "The Best Catch There Is," in his book *Doings and Undoings,* argues that Heller accurately and artistically describes the "gigantic insane asylum" of life in the mid-twentieth century.[13]

By 1964 the novel was not just being regarded as a blip in publishing history, or merely as commentary on the issues of the day, but as literature. Given the still predominant realistic canon of late modernism, a number of scholars took on the matter of *Catch-22*'s place in literary history. Viewing the book as a manifestation of the relatively new trends in black humor and the absurd, Ihab Hassan included *Catch-22* in several articles concerning black humor as an affirmation of life,[14] while Joseph J. Waldmeir found the novel a magnificent example of the absurd, though flawed in its superficial complexity, very real repetitiveness, and "totally unconvincing" ending.[15] Constance Denniston considered the novel as a "romance-parody," and Englishman G. B. McK. Henry as a Dickensian "tragic-farce" blending serious literary concerns with motifs, some unfortunate, from popular entertainment; both sought thus to explain the two-dimensional characters and chaotic structure.[16] Sanford Pinsker and Vance Ramsey focused on the character of Yossarian, Pinsker seeing him as an eternal innocent in the Huck Finn tradition of American protagonists, and Ramsey considering him as an antihero in an insane world.[17]

Over the next ten years others pursued like generic considerations and comparisons. Caroline Gordon and Jeanne Richardson placed Heller's absurdity against Lewis Carroll's and found him a trifle wanting; Brian Way regarded the book as a brilliant blend of the traditions of absurdism and radical social protest, and saw it as a turning point in American literature.[18] J. P. Stern compared *Catch-22* to Jaroslav Hasek's antic anti-World War I novel *The Good Soldier Schweik*.[19] At the end of its first decade, *Catch-22* was considered as a social-surrealist novel by Jesse Ritter, as a war novel by Eric Solomon and others, as a "mock epic" by Victor J. Milne, and as satire in classical modes updated by Northrop Frye, Menippean (Jess Ritter) and Juvenalian (James Nagel).[20] Critics such as John W. Hunt and Eugene McNamara continued to argue for *Catch-22*'s inclusion in the literature of the absurd, Hamlin Hill and Max F. Schulz for the novel as an example of black humor; while Bruce Janoff saw the problem of the ending as a result of the confusion of the two sub-genres.[21] Nelvin Vos and James

E. Miller published works, in 1967 and 1968, respectively, that also tied Heller's work to new American trends in the literature of the absurd.[22]

In the late sixties other threads began to separate from the skein of *Catch-22* criticism. The moral development of the novel and of its main character in particular formed the core of Minna Doskow's "The Night Journey in *Catch-22*."[23] Others commented on the moral orthodoxy of the book, supporting positions contrary to the earliest assumptions that it attacked conventional morality. Essays by Victor J. Milne and Jim Castelli, both published in 1970, argued for Christian interpretations of Yossarian's character; Wayne Charles Miller, in his book *An Armed American: Its Face in Fiction*, viewed Yossarian as a "symbol of humanistic faith"; and in a 1974 essay Daniel Walden explained the novel and its hero in traditional Jewish terms.[24]

The question of the novel's structure received new attention in the late sixties as well. James L. McDonald and James M. Mellard investigated the plot from the standpoint of doubling and déjà vu; Jan Solomon attempted to show that two time lines exist in the novel, one a cyclical one revolving around Yossarian, and another, cutting impossibly and absurdly across the first, featuring Milo.[25] In 1970 Doug Gaukroger correctly showed that Solomon had misread the book and proposed his own chronology.[26] Refinements on the novel's structure continued with Thomas Allen Nelson's 1971 essay on cyclical development of episodes and themes and with Howard J. Stark's 1973 article on déjà vu.[27] Another 1973 analysis of the chronology of the story by Clinton S. Burhans included a full outline of the plot, complete with dates and a few mistakes, both Heller's and his own.[28] This discussion continues up to the present, with Robert Merrill's 1986 essay "The Structure and Meaning of *Catch-22*."[29] (For more words on this issue, and perhaps even the last word, see chapter 4.)

A new flurry of popular interest came to Joseph Heller at the cusp of the sixties and seventies with the productions, albeit short-running, of his two plays *We Bombed in New Haven* and *Catch-22: A Dramatization* and with the appearance of the Mike Nichols movie based on the novel. As distaste for the war in Vietnam spread from college campuses to the nation at large, so did interest in Heller's work, and shortly after Nichols's film the novel finally reached the best-seller list in America. Heller had proved an amiable and informative interview subject in the immediate aftermath of *Catch-22*—most usefully in his 1962 interview with Paul Krassner for *The Realist*[30]—and print and electronic media alike took advantage of that fact during this period.

The most valuable of the later interviews, such as those in *Paris Review, Studies in the Novel,* and *Playboy,* confirmed a number of the critics' speculations.[31] Besides filling in biographical details regarding Heller's Coney Island background and his war experiences, these interviews have provided a good record of Heller's literary influences and his intentions in writing *Catch-22*. Defending himself against charges that he minimized the importance of winning World War II, Heller noted that he fought the war with enthusiasm and emphasized anew that he was really writing about the cold war that followed, with its anticommunist purges and its smug hypocrisies. He also underlined those passages in the novel where he stresses that Yossarian is embracing his responsibilities as a moral man, not deserting them. Leading questions from interviewers about the novel's structure also produced confirmation of critics' observations about doubling and déjà vu.

Heller's appearances in the media increased with the publication of *Something Happened,* which was an immediate best-seller even though most reviewers expressed disappointment with it. Inevitably critics and readers compared Heller's second novel to his first, drawing attention to those factors that had made the first so significant. Like *Catch-22, Something Happened* was often criticized for being too long and redundant, while furthermore lacking the vitiating humor, action, and absurdity of its predecessor. Its satire was more gloomy and introspective and narrowly focused on "the organization man."

If some commentators expressed doubts about Heller's general artistry, *Catch-22*'s stature remained unshaken. In fact, the period of the second novel's appearance represented a climax in *Catch-22* criticism. The year 1973 saw at least two major contributions: Robert M. Scotto's *Catch-22: A Critical Edition*—including several reprinted articles and the excised chapter "Love, Dad"—and A "Catch-22" Casebook, a collection of reviews, interviews, and articles, both previously published and original, edited by Frederick Kiley and Walter McDonald.[32] In the following year there appeared yet another collection of reprints and originals, Critical Essays on "Catch-22," edited by James Nagel.[33] In that year Joseph Weixlmann also published "A Bibliography of Joseph Heller's Catch-22."[34]

In the mid-seventies critics were still refining and redefining familiar discussions of the novel's generic classification, cyclical and satirical technique, absurdity, and ethical stance. Even the matter of the novel's worth appeared to be not wholly settled; an essay by H. R. Swardson in College English complained that in retrospect Catch-22 was sentimental and "phony."[35] Nagel took a relatively new direction, however, by examining Heller's notes and papers stored at Brandeis University and publishing two articles about the earlier drafts of the novel.[36] The growing fashion in linguistic and deconstructive criticism began to show up in commentary on Catch-22 in the late seventies. Along these lines are articles by Carol Pearson, Gary W. Davis, and Adam J. Sorkin about the destructive or deceptive use of language by authority and institutions in the novel, and, tangentially, Fred M. Fetrow's discussion of Heller's use of names.[37]

As the eighties approached, a generation of critics emerged who had grown up with the novel as students in the sixties. With increasing hindsight, the novel came to be appreciated not only as a harbinger of the postmodern literary movement that arose in that decade (Jerome Klinkowitz) but as an artifact of the social and political culture of that revolutionary era as well (Morris Dickstein).[38] Any student of Heller's perusing much of the criticism circa 1980, however, begins to experience déjà vu: much of it continues to circle around the issues of absurdity, morality, genre, and structure. In bringing together the issues of absurdity and morality, Leon F. Seltzer's "Milo's 'Culpable Innocence': Absurdity as Moral Insanity in Catch-22" is one of the more useful essays of the period.[39]

The eighties have seen two more novels by Joseph Heller—Good as Gold and God Knows—as well as one nonfiction book, No Laugh-

ing Matter, concerning his bout with Guillain-Barré syndrome. All were best-sellers but in the main critical disappointments. If they added little to the author's repute, however, they took little away from *Catch-22*. The scholars who have addressed Heller's later work seriously have dealt inevitably with the subjects of satire and humor, and with the new issue of ethnicity that the author has embraced after resolutely avoiding it in his first two novels. More books and articles now view Heller's career as a whole through comparative studies of his works. Commentary on his first novel, however, continues at the very least to equal that on all the rest of his writings combined. *Catch-22* promises to dominate Heller criticism and the author's literary reputation for some time to come.

A Reading

4

Method in Madness, Part I

It is difficult to approach the study of *Catch-22* without first coming to terms with its structure. Anyone who has read beyond the novel's first chapter quickly becomes aware of its lack of a traditional chronological plot. Indeed, one of the most frequent complaints made by early reviewers was that the novel was formless and chaotic, and many blamed Heller for not exercising more artistic control over his materials. For the *New York Times Book Review* the novel "gasps for want of craft and sensibility"; the *New Yorker* agreed that the book was not even a novel and argued, "It doesn't even seem to have been written; instead it gives the impression of having been shouted onto paper."[40] Even sympathetic reviewers gave in on this point, although defending the novel's formlessness on the grounds that it is consistent with the chaotic cosmos and lunatic logic of the story.

When academic critics began to give Heller's book a closer look, the issue of structure arose as an early concern. A close analysis of the narrative revealed that it does in fact have organization of a sort, albeit an intricate one, and that beneath the apparent chaos of the story line exists a coherent sequence of events. Relatively few, however—indeed, a mere handful—have attempted to unravel Heller's complicated chronology, and all so far have fallen victim to some degree to the rhetorical traps Heller sets in the narrative to foil such attempts.

The first such serious endeavor to unravel *Catch-22*'s meticulously snarled skein was Jan Solomon's 1967 article "The Structure of Joseph Heller's *Catch-22*."[41] Solomon maintains that two opposing time lines dominate the novel. One is the cyclical pattern of most of the novel, rooted in Yossarian's psychological perception of events. Yossarian's world is one of increasing moral decay, with suggestions of existentialist absurdism, and the dizzy nature of the narrative reflects this fact. On the other hand, Milo Minderbinder's history progresses in "the solid fashion of nineteenth-century fiction"[42]; he begins as an ambitious mess hall officer and ends up dominating the world.

According to Solomon, Milo's linear time line cuts across Yossarian's cyclical time line in a manner patently impossible. For example, he maintains that Milo and Yossarian are introduced only after Yossarian's hospital visit of chapter 1, and thus after Avignon, Snowden, and the Great Big Siege of Bologna. This is of course causally impossible, since Yossarian and Milo appear together in the tree at Snowden's funeral, and a number of Milo's earlier dealings, such as the cornering of the Egyptian cotton market and his subsequent contracts with the Germans, take place when he already knows Yossarian.

Solomon cites these and other examples as evidence that Heller intends Milo and Yossarian to operate on absurdly contradictory time lines, and he argues that it is Heller's intent thus to make a thematic point: Yossarian is trapped within the illogical circles of his world, while Milo, operating successfully according to its mad rules, progresses inexorably to ultimate triumph.

Unfortunately, Solomon reaches his conclusion on a faulty assessment of the chronology, as noted by Doug Gaukroger a few years later in his article "Time Structure in *Catch-22*."[43] Gaukroger dispenses entirely with Solomon's incorrect reading of the narrative and does a reasonably good job of establishing the true sequence of the novel's major events, based on a painstaking analysis of the text. In a long plot summary, he correctly sets in order the main bombing campaigns of the plot—respectively, Ferrara, Bologna, and Avignon—and weaves the careers of Yossarian, Milo, and the other major characters through them. In this way he does discover a couple of errors on Heller's part, which will be noted in their proper place later in this discussion.

Although Gaukroger's time line has proved accurate enough to serve as the basis for most subsequent discussions of chronology, he does make a couple of errors himself. For instance, he has Milo buying the Egyptian cotton crop and arranging his deals with the Germans during the Bologna campaign, instead of before it; he also has the novel beginning when Yossarian has thirty-eight missions instead of forty-four, an assumption picked up by Clinton S. Burhans, Jr., in his 1973 article.[44]

Burhans's contribution to the discussion of structure is a revised chronology with dates. He begins with Yossarian's entrance into the army sometime in 1941, followed by his transfer to the air corps that same year; his first Thanksgiving in the hospital while a private at Lowery Field, Colorado, thus takes place in November 1941, and his Thanksgiving in bed with Mrs. Scheisskopf, therefore, one year later, in 1942. By this scheme Yossarian reaches Pianosa before September 1943, when Burhans has him at twenty-three missions at the time of Colonel Cathcart's appearance.

The chronology becomes more detailed after April 1944 and the foundation of Milo's syndicate. According to Burhans, Milo arranges the Orvieto deal in April; Ferrara and Bologna both take place in May; Avignon and the death of Snowden transpire in June, and the first chapter opens in July. From there on the major events of the last third of the book unfold, ending with Yossarian's desertion in December 1944.

Utilizing his chronology, Burhans points out what he sees as errors in Heller's planning. He is troubled by the long, six-month gap between September 1943, when he has Cathcart appear, and April 1944, when most of the story begins; he finds it incredible that Yossarian would only fly nine missions in that time and that Cathcart would only raise those required by ten. Also, he notes that according to the narrative Milo bombed the squadron only seven months after Yossarian left cadet training, whereas his chronology shows a gap of a couple of years between these events—according to Burhans, a clear error on Heller's part.

Later commentator Robert Merrill, however, correctly notes that Burhans himself errs in at least two places.[45] First of all, the mission of Orvieto, where Milo contracts with both the Allied and Axis forces and where Mudd, the dead man in Yossarian's tent, dies, takes place after Milo's disastrous cornering of the Egyptian cotton market, not before it, as Burhans's chronology shows; Orvieto, like the bombing of the squadron, is prompted, after all, by Milo's expensive error in judgment. Furthermore, Merrill correctly notes, during Yossarian's visit to the hospital with which the novel opens, he has forty-four missions, not thirty-eight, as Gaukroger and Burhans both allege.

Burhans's problems with the six-month gap can also be explained by errors on his, not Heller's part—errors that Merrill fails to note. This gap exists because Burhans unaccountably places the beginning of Yossarian's World War II career early in 1941; thus Burhans has him malingering in the hospital in Lowery Field over Thanksgiving of that year and complaining to Wintergreen and others that the war is not proceeding fast enough to end before his training does. But the United States did not even enter World War II until the bombing of Pearl Harbor on 7 December 1941! It is not at all likely that Yossarian would be training for combat months before America even declared war. Far more logical, and historical, would be to begin Yossarian's training in 1942; doing so also matches Heller's real-life wartime history, which was the basis for Yossarian's.

All of the discussions of chronology cited above have worked directly out of Heller's admittedly difficult and convoluted text. Surprisingly, no critic has taken much advantage of one set of evidence that was publicly provided with the publication in 1973 of the essay collection A "Catch-22" Casebook, edited by Frederick Kiley and Walter McDonald: facsimiles of the charts that Heller himself created on desk blotter paper in the final stages of Catch-22's composition. Though not every episode of the novel is accounted for in the sections of the charts visible in the book, Heller's intentions are clear for many of the most important characters, and particularly Yossarian. While these charts are not wholly infallible, they do help solve some of the difficulties that the critics have fallen into by trying to tease the chronology out of the text alone, and they do endorse certain interpretations of the chronology over others.

The charts are organized with a time line running vertically along the left edge and a list of characters extending along the top edge at the head of several columns. Yossarian has the first three columns, followed to the right by a column for Dunbar and McWatt, one for Clevinger and Nately, one for Hungry Joe and Dobbs, one for Orr, another for Milo, and so on through the chaplain, the majors, the colonels, the generals, the doctors, the nurses, and others. The time line begins with Yossarian leaving civilian life for basic training at Lowery Field, Colorado, where he meets Wintergreen and discovers the hospital as a refuge from calisthenics. The chart offers no dates at this point, but for the reasons noted above the first hospital stay must take place in 1942; Thanksgiving 1943, therefore, finds him stationed as an air cadet in Santa Ana, California, and arguing about God with Scheisskopf's wife. Heller does date Yossarian's arrival on Pianosa, placing it in "early 1944," well after the September 1943 date set by Burhans. According to the chart, Yossarian flies twenty-three missions before Colonel Cathcart arrives, also in early 1944, and raises the required missions to thirty.

In March, according to Heller's time line, occurs the mission to Ferrara, where Aarfy's incompetence forces Yossarian to go over the bridge twice before destroying it. Milo forms his cartel in April, and Cathcart raises the missions to thirty-five. On 4 June 1944, the Allies enter Rome—a historical fact noted on the chart—and Yossarian accompanies Nately to the Roman whorehouse where Nately falls in love with his whore.

In late June the Great Big Siege of Bologna takes place, with all of its attendant episodes. Immediately thereafter Yossarian takes his rest leave in Rome with thirty-two missions behind him and meets Luciana. He returns to his unit and heads directly for the hospital when Cathcart raises the missions to forty. Here is where some scholars have become confused: no sooner does Yossarian leave the hospital than, according to the chart, Cathcart raises the missions to forty-five and Yossarian, now with only thirty-eight missions, enters the hospital a second time within this narrow interval.

The mission over Avignon, and thus Snowden's death, takes place in July, as do Snowden's funeral and Yossarian's receipt of a medal in the nude. About the time Cathcart orders fifty missions, Clevinger disappears inside a cloud. Yossarian returns to the hospital at the beginning of August, "in despair over Clevinger's death," according to the chart. He has forty-four missions at this point, and it is here, when he meets the chaplain, that the first chapter of the novel takes place. After this stay Yossarian begs Daneeka to ground him, and the chaplain takes Yossarian's case to Cathcart during their discussion of the *Saturday Evening Post*.

In September, according to Heller's chart, the missions required go to fifty-five, and Yossarian, with forty-eight missions, pleads with Daneeka again; he reaches fifty-one just before Cathcart raises the required missions to sixty, at which point Yossarian tackles Major Major. Shortly thereafter Yossarian is wounded in the thigh on the milk run over Parma. While convalescing in the hospital he gooses Nurse Duckett, which begins their affair, and has his interview with the psychiatrist Major Sanderson. Over the following month, Orr disappears, McWatt accidentally chops Kid Sampson in half and commits suicide, and the missions are raised to sixty-five and then seventy.

Mid-October finds Yossarian in Rome again, where he helps Nately rescue his whore from the "big shots," at which time she finally falls in love with Nately. The following month Yossarian breaks Nately's nose at the raucous Thanksgiving celebration during which Sergeant Knight sprays the camp with a machine gun. Yossarian and Dunbar lie their way into the hospital to visit Nately, where they are joined by the chaplain. During this stay the soldier in white returns, driving Dunbar crazy, and Dunbar is disappeared.

By early December Yossarian and Nately have flown seventy missions. After Milo expresses his wish to get combat credit, Cathcart boots them up to eighty, and Nately, wishing to remain near his whore, volunteers to continue. After Nately and Dobbs collide mid-air, killing both crews, Yossarian refuses to fly more missions. The remainder of the plot unfolds in December 1944: the chaplain's trial, Peckem's fleeting triumph over Dreedle and Scheisskopf's promotion, Yossarian's AWOL flight to "the Eternal City," Nately's whore's assaults on his life, Korn's deal, and Yossarian's desertion upon hearing of Orr's arrival in Sweden.

For the most part, Heller's charts explain the book's chronology better than do the scholars who have limited themselves to textual evidence. Even using the charts, however, one discovers that Heller did make some errors, though not as many as his critics think. Some errors are the result of apparent last-minute changes, such as the time of Milo's arrival to the squadron. According to the text, Milo is unaware of the incident wherein the mess sergeant, Corporal Snark, poisoned the men with laundry soap during the Ferrara campaign (65). The charts, however, show Milo arriving well before March, when Ferrara took place. Heller has Yossarian and Milo meet for the first time in the spring of 1944 (61–62), before Milo sets up his cartel in April. One of the first subjects they discuss, however, is Nately, his whore, and the old man who lives in her brothel in Rome. Since Rome did not fall into Allied hands until June 4, we have a patent impossibility here, inconsistent with the story line.

But the chart helps explain away another "error" noted by Burhans and seconded by Merrill regarding Major ——— de Coverley's promotion of Milo to mess officer.[46] Both see Heller as erring in having the Major promote Milo upon his triumphal return from Rome in early June after having secured the whore-filled apartments, even though Milo clearly had his cartel going in April. Looking at the relevant text (138–139), one can see where they got the idea, since the promotion takes place immediately after a description of the Major's visit to Rome and his new eyepatch. But in Heller's complex narrative, juxtaposition in space does not necessarily mean juxtaposition in time; the transitional lines in no way insist that what follows in the text must follow in the story's chronology. Between the description of the Major's Roman excursion and his appointment of Milo stands only the statement, "To the men in the squadron, Major ——— de Coverley was a colossus, though they never dared tell him so. The only one who ever did dare address him was Milo Minderbinder, who approached the horseshoe-pitching pit with a hard-boiled egg his second week in the squadron and held it aloft for Major ———— de Coverley to see" (138). Nothing in this passage suggests explicitly or implicitly that it happens after the fall of Rome described just above it.

Merrill makes a similar mistake when he claims Heller erred because chapters 2 and 17 refer to the same hospital visits, even though in chapter 2 Yossarian has forty-four missions, while in chapter 17 he is rushing into the hospital "determined to remain [there] forever rather than fly one mission more" than thirty-eight (169). Once more a critical reader has been fooled by a narrative bridge; between this paragraph in chapter 17 and the reappearance of the soldier in white are nearly two pages that concern hospitals in general and death, with specific reference to Snowden and Clevinger. In fact, one sees from Heller's chart that Snowden and Clevinger both meet their ends *between* Yossarian's hospital visit at thirty-eight missions (in late June) and his visit "that last time" (171) at forty-four (in August). These intervening paragraphs thus serve as a transition between the two visits, which Merrill, among others, incorrectly sees as the same visit.

On the other hand, other anomalies that scholars have noted *do* represent oversights on Heller's part. Beside the impossibility of Yossarian and Milo discussing Nately's whore at their introduction is Appleby's prompt visit to squadron commander Major Major, as soon as he and Yossarian arrive on Pianosa, to report Yossarian's refusal to take his Atabrine tablets. Here Appleby is humiliated when Sergeant Towser, following Major Major's orders, refuses to admit him until Major Major leaves his office. But this episode is impossible within the chronology: Major Major does not go into hiding until after Colonel Cathcart promotes him to squadron commander, and Colonel Cathcart does not arrive on Pianosa until after the death of Colonel Nevers, at which time Appleby and Yossarian have been on the island long enough for Yossarian to have flown twenty-three missions. Major Major is thus simply another pilot at the time Yossarian and Appleby arrive, and not yet a reclusive squadron commander.

It is of course possible that the author tossed in a few such impossibilities to underline the absurdity of his story, though, as his notes and charts demonstrate, he otherwise did a painstaking job of setting the episodes straight. Combining these notes and charts with close textual analysis does iron out most of the chronology; nonetheless, between the difficult texture of the narrative and the few errors, intentional or not, that Heller does make, no time line will perfectly account for every single one of the intersections of character and event in the novel. A substantially accurate chart of the major events in the novel, however, has been appended to the end of this study for ready reference; it is based on Heller's own chart but fine-tuned to eliminate some textual anomalies, particularly in Milo's history.

The main value of this exercise is twofold: it gives us a reliable framework for discussing the important episodes of the story, and it proves that, contrary to the complaints of early critics and new readers, *Catch-22* is not simply chaotic, but meticulously written to *appear* chaotic, as Heller has insisted in a number of interviews. It is in fact a painstakingly constructed book.

Why, then, did Heller go to so much trouble to confuse the time sense of the plot? And are there some overarching principles and patterns of organization behind the apparent chaos?

THE STRUCTURE OF *CATCH-22*

Several critics have addressed these very questions, including—not surprisingly—those who have wrestled with the chronology. Some, like Jan Solomon and James M. Mellard, see the confusion in the time scheme as reflective of Yossarian's psychological disorientation and moral development. The dominant early consensus runs a bit broader, as expressed by Doug Gaukroger: "The unorthodox treatment of time in *Catch-22* is both parallel to, and prepares the reader for, the unorthodox treatment of the subject matter. It is only fitting that a novel which deals with an apparently absurd and confused world should be written in an apparently absurd and confused style."[47]

Critics soon found, however, that there are patterns in the novel that ameliorate this apparent confusion. A favorite pattern, and one that has the advantage of being endorsed by Heller himself, is the motif of déjà vu.[48] Déjà vu—the feeling of having experienced something before—is considered expressly and at great length by Chaplain Tappman in those chapters at the novel's midpoint that feature him. But the reader shares this sense throughout the novel, too. As Heller and critics such as Mellard and James L. McDonald have noted, the reader almost never receives the full text of an episode at its first mention. Characters and scenes recur, and each time they do the narrative adds more information. As McDonald phrases it, "The past event . . . is seldom related as one complete, coherent unit. Rather the reader learns of it partially, in disjointed fragments. . . . Only tentatively and gradually can he reconstruct it, place it in relation to other events in time, and understand its significance."[49]

Examples so abound that one need only turn the pages of the book to find them everywhere, pullulating like insect eggs. The most frequently identified, however, and those which seem representative of the thematic significance of these repetitions, are the soldier in white, the hospital, and Snowden's death. Not only does the reader learn more as such episodes repeat, but the general tone of each subsequent repetition tends to darken. Thus, for instance, when we first see Yossarian in the hospital, he is whimsically censoring letters while merrily malingering, and the soldier in white is a ridiculous figure that provides Yossarian and Dunbar with an excuse to goad the Texan. But in chapter 17 the same scene in the hospital leads to a discussion of death, disease, injustice, and the meaninglessness of the universe, and the last hospital episodes of the novel find Yossarian twice wounded and Dunbar driven mad by the soldier in white, who is no longer droll but horrifying. The increasing significance of the Snowden scenes, growing in horror as they gradually grow in detail, should be evident to anyone who has read the book.

Heller's own avowed scheme for the structure of the novel suggests that, the repetition and déjà vu aside, he sees the story built around three main missions—Ferrara, Bologna, and Avignon.[50] Furthermore, the first four-fifths of the novel, roughly speaking, are meant to create "the effect of something being chaotic and anarchistic"; the events come together into a coherent whole and assume forward motion only near the end, when Yossarian makes his decision to desert.[51] Given the novel's incremental darkening of tone, cyclical repetition of scenes in the hospital and elsewhere, and the gradual development of Yossarian's moral consciousness—all matters that will be expanded upon in their proper places below—scholars have sought logical divisions within the story, coherent blocks of narrative bounded by these alterations in tone, thematic considerations, or character development.

The hospital scenes have provided one such set of divisions. Based on them, Jan Solomon introduced a threefold development in the novel. His first division begins with Yossarian's hospital stay in the first chapter, embraces the early descriptions of life on Pianosa and Yossarian's friends, the Siege of Bologna and Yossarian's affair with Luciana, and ends with Yossarian's return to the hospital as Colonel Cathcart raises the missions to forty at the end of chapter 16. Solomon's second division begins with the hospital and the soldier in white again in chapter 17 and continues through the next roughly one third of the novel, dealing with Cathcart and the chaplain, the mission to Avignon, and Nately's whore, and ends with Yossarian's wound in the thigh and his return to the hospital, covered in chapters 26 and 27. For Solomon, the last third of the novel thus begins with chapter 28, in which Orr disappears; it concentrates on the present, except for the flashbacks to Snowden, and the increasing horrors that lead to Yossarian's final decision.

Merrill, the latest to attempt such divisions, favors a scheme similar to Solomon's, except that he marks each third with the appearance of the soldier in white, at chapters 1, 17, and 34, noting the deepening of thematic importance and darkening of narrative tone that accompany each of these reappearances.

Burhans, also on the basis of tone, recommends yet another threefold division, with chapters 1 through 28 offering the lightest comic touch, chapters 29 through 39 being dominated by horrors, and the remaining three chapters turning toward hope and guarded optimism.

Onto this framework he superimposes a second set of five divisions related to subplots, with chapters 1 through 10 establishing the narrative present, chapters 11 through 16 handling the Great Big Siege of Bologna, chapters 17 through 21 continuing in the narrative present, chapters 22 through 24 digressing for Milo's subplot, and the remainder of the book finishing chronologically in the main plot, with side trips to the subplot of Peckem's war with Dreedle.

Howard J. Stark suggests another threefold division, with breaks between chapters 18 and 19, and 25 and 26. Stark asserts, in the wake of others, that the chaplain's vus—not just déjà vu but *presque vu* and *jamais vu*—provide "the key to the structural method and pattern of the novel."[52] But instead of bringing the narrative full circle every time to the hospital or the soldier in white, each division according to Stark circles back to its own starting point. His first third thus begins and ends with Yossarian in the hospital, a period embracing four weeks in real time but meandering back over events of the previous two years; the second section is framed by the chaplain's visit to Colonel Cathcart, and the remaining seventeen chapters finish the story more or less chronologically, with only the final recurrence of Snowden's death still providing the motif of déjà vu.

Actually, considering the large number of overlapping cycles, and cycles within cycles, in the novel, any attempt to break the narrative up into logical units ultimately proves arbitrary to some degree, all protestations to the contrary notwithstanding. All the scholars mentioned above have provided excellent rationales for their own schemes, but whether these rationales are also the author's is another question.

Fortunately, it is possible to take the general consensus on the alterations of tone and the presence of déjà vu cycles, add these factors to Heller's insistence on the importance of the central missions, and come up with another set of divisions rooted not only in tone, chronology, and repetition, but also in the changing prevalence of certain characters, incidents, settings, and themes. This scheme provides five sections of roughly equal length, which—if also arguably arbitrary—permit a more detailed and orderly discussion of the novel than the formidable chunks of seventeen or twenty-five chapters that most schemes create. The rest of this study, therefore, will be built around the following divisions.

The first section embraces the first nine chapters, which focus on Yossarian's immediate circle in Pianosa. It begins, as noted earlier, with his hospital visit at forty-four missions and circles mostly around the late summer period of Avignon and the deaths of Snowden and Clevinger, though little is said of these events. In flashbacks it reaches back to spring—to Ferrara and the beginning of Milo's activities— back one year to Lieutenant Scheisskopf and Clevinger at Santa Ana, and back a lifetime to pick up the history of Major Major Major.

The second section begins with Clevinger's death and the announcement of the campaign to Bologna in chapter 10. The chapter maintains the mad, chaotic tone of the first section, though the first major darkening appears when the pall of morbidity settles on the base during the Great Big Siege of Bologna. In fact, Bologna dominates this section, despite digressions to episodes from the recent past—Captain Black's Glorious Loyalty Oath campaign, Luciana, and (again) Ferrara and Milo's beginnings. This section circles back to the hospital, where it ends, in chapters 17 and 18, with further flashbacks to Lowery Field and Santa Ana. The dominance of the hospital motif and the campaign to Bologna in these chapters brings to the forefront the questions of death and cosmic justice.

The third section begins with chapter 19 and Colonel Cathcart, as he receives the chaplain to discuss the *Saturday Evening Post*; it is August, shortly after the chaplain's visit to Yossarian described in chapter 1. Chapters 19 through 25, bridging the midpoint of the novel, feature in large part viewpoints other than Yossarian's, and offer an interplay of characters who reflect the different value systems of the novel—Colonel Cathcart, Chaplain Tappman, and Milo Minderbinder, as well as the important discussion of idealism and survivalism that takes place between Nately and the Old Man in the brothel. Flashbacks revolve mainly around the mission to Avignon, from Yossarian's moaning in the briefing room through his refusal to wear a uniform at Snowden's funeral. This section ends after coming back full circle to the chaplain and Colonel Cathcart.

The fourth section begins with chapter 26, in which Yossarian receives his wound in the thigh and a legitimate return to the hospital. From here on the narrative of the novel is for the most part chronological. This section alternates between Yossarian's increasingly serious fear of death, as one by one his "pals" are destroyed, Nately's affair with his whore, and Peckem's struggle to win control of combat operations from General Dreedle. The action switches between Pianosa and Rome, where Nately's whore lives and where Peckem has moved his command. It ends with chapter 37 and Peckem's triumph, which he promptly loses upon learning that Scheisskopf has been promoted over him. These chapters reinforce and expand upon the themes developed in the earlier groupings.

The fifth section, then, is made up of the final, "serious" chapters of the novel, those that represent the alteration in tone and in Yossarian's character that has bothered so many critics. It begins with Yossarian's refusal to fly any more missions, moves through the climactic "Eternal City" chapter, and ends with Yossarian's rejection of Korn's "odious deal" and his decision to desert.

The internal coherence of each of these divisions—and the usefulness of this structural scheme as a whole—should become more apparent as the sections are treated separately in the discussion to follow. In addition, each grouping of chapters will provide a springboard for leaping into the various issues that Catch-22 considers and the techniques that Heller uses to develop them.

5

Pianosa: Method in Madness, Part 2

The first section of the novel takes place for the most part on the U. S. Air Force base on the Mediterranean island of Pianosa. It begins with Yossarian malingering in the hospital following Clevinger's disappearance; it is late August, the number of required missions is fifty, and Yossarian has forty-four. It is during this visit to the hospital that Yossarian meets the Texan, the soldier in white, and Chaplain Tappman. In the chapters that follow, the narrative introduces the reader to Yossarian's peers on the base—Dunbar and McWatt, Clevinger and Nately, Havermeyer and Appleby, Hungry Joe and Chief White Halfoat, Orr and others. By reference or anecdote, most of the other characters in the chain of command are also introduced here: the doctors Daneeka and Stubbs, Captain Black, Majors ———— de Coverley and Major Major, Colonels Cathcart and Korn, Generals Peckem and Dreedle. Much of the action circles around the time of Clevinger's disappearance, though the event itself is not expressly mentioned until chapter 10; most, though not all, of Yossarian's attempts to get grounded follow his return from the hospital visit of chapter 1 after Clevinger's disappearance, while the arguments between Yossarian and Clevinger outlined in chapter 2 immediately precede the event.

This section contains some important flashbacks as well. It returns to Lowery Field, Colorado, where the military career of Yossarian begins along with those of Wintergreen and Chief White Halfoat, and to cadet school in Santa Ana, where Lieutenant Scheisskopf plans parades while Yossarian and the other cadets sleep with his wife, and where Scheisskopf brings charges against Clevinger that lead to the latter's absurd interrogation. Chapter 5 offers the first extended versions of both Catch-22 and Snowden's death, though both are mentioned in passing earlier; chapter 7 goes back to the first meeting of Yossarian and Milo Minderbinder on Pianosa and the foundation of Milo's business enterprise. This first group of chapters builds up to two well-remembered set pieces of the novel: Clevinger's interrogation in chapter 8 and the story of Major Major Major Major in chapter 9.

It is widely agreed that the first few chapters of *Catch-22* are generally lighter in tone than those that follow. Despite the background of the war, and the almost casual deaths in the hospital and outside it, the events and style of these chapters are blatantly, even insistently, comic. Among early reviewers, some complained that the humor was too insistent and not even funny. In the anonymous and highly negative *Daedalus* review cited above, Roger H. Smith insists that the wit in the novel not only flaunts itself but is also limited to only two forms: direct contradiction and echolalia, by which he means verbal repetition. Most of the examples he cites to make his case come from the first nine chapters, and in fact it is here that these devices are most obvious. Smith also protests that certain comic images, such as the soldier in white being fed his own urine, are too disjunctive in subject and tone, and thus too disgusting to be comic.

Other early commentators—among them Robert Protherough and Jean Kennard—recognized further comic devices: the surprise substitute word, usually contradictory ("Yossarian had stopped playing chess with him because the games were so interesting they were foolish" [9].), the deflation or unexpected reversal of a familiar cliché or attitude ("Colonel Cathcart had courage and never hesitated to volunteer his men for any target available" [57].), the disparity of subject and tone ("The colonel was in Communications, and he was kept busy day and night transmitting glutinous messages from the interior into square pads of gauze. . ." [15].), and the presentation of meaningless or optionless choices ("'The men don't *have* to sign Piltchard and Wren's loyalty oath if they don't want to. But we need you to starve them to death if they don't'" [118].).

Repetition, contradiction and oxymoron, deflation of accepted (or clichéd) attitudes, the misjoinder of subject and tone, choiceless choices—all appear with great frequency in the text of this section. One need only turn to the first page or two of the novel to begin to find ample examples of these rhetorical devices. The well-known opening lines of the book, for instance, offer a cliché ("It was love at first sight."), which is promptly deflated ("The first time Yossarian saw the chaplain he fell madly in love with him."). The following paragraph discusses Yossarian's liver condition, repeating "jaundice" in each of five sentences. This paragraph, describing the pain that falls just short of being jaundice and thus confuses the doctors, is cited by Protherough as a low-level example of a meaningless choice.

Soon to follow are other repetitive passages, such as Yossarian's first conversation with the chaplain, which begins with Yossarian insisting he feels "pretty good":

> "That's good," said the chaplain.
> "Yes," Yossarian said. "Yes, that is good."
> "I meant to come around sooner," the chaplain said, "but I really haven't been well."
> "That's too bad," Yossarian said.
> "Just a head cold," the chaplain added quickly.
> "I've got a fever of a hundred and one," Yossarian added just as quickly.
> "That's too bad," said the chaplain.
> "Yes," Yossarian agreed. "Yes, that is too bad." (12)

Their discussion continues with nearly every statement made by one of them being echoed by the other, climaxing in:

> "You're a chaplain," he exclaimed ecstatically. "I didn't know you were a chaplain."

"Why, yes," the chaplain answered. "Didn't you know I was a chaplain?"

"Why, no. I didn't know you were a chaplain." (13)

The initial chapter also provides several direct contradictions, such as "The Texan turned out to be good-natured, generous and likable. In three days no one could stand him" (10), and "'Nately had a bad start. He came from a good family'" (13). It also presents a striking example of conflict of subject and tone in the figure cited by Smith as being revolting for that very reason: the soldier in white. Just how thick and fast these and other devices appear in the early chapters becomes evident with close reading of the text. At the risk of excessive repetition, let us scrutinize a single chapter, the short second chapter, "Clevinger," as a springboard to that end.

Chapter 2 begins with a free-associative bridge from the previous chapter: the CID man mentioned in the last sentence there leads to "In a way the C.I.D. man was pretty lucky, because outside the hospital the war was still going on" (16). With that the CID man drops out of sight in favor of the war. The same thing happens at the beginning of the following paragraph: "But Yossarian couldn't be happy, even though the Texan didn't want him to be, because outside the hospital there was still nothing funny going on" (16–17). At this point the Texan also gives way to the war.

Such sudden transitions are more surprising than comic and have much to do with the delirious feel of the narrative. They are all that is left of the more modernist free association à la James Joyce that was characteristic of the novel's earliest version (according to Frederick Karl, "Evidently strongly influenced by *Ulysses,* Heller had originally tried to make the narrative typically Joycean: that is, full of intermittent streams of consciousness and involutions of time."[53]). They can contribute some humorous effects, however, especially in those frequent instances in which they take place mid-sentence or combine with other clauses that suggest nonsensical contradictions or reversals, as in the last sentence quoted above.

At this stage of the narrative, such non sequitur and even self-negating transitions are used for quick characterization and foreshadowing as well. A couple of pages into this chapter, for instance, appear a pair of paragraphs that briefly describe Yossarian's fellow fliers in a series of long, complex sentences full of internal transitions, contradictions, and surprises. At the end of learning about the tent Yossarian shares with Orr, we read "Orr rolled up the side flaps to allow a breeze that never blew to flush away the air baking inside" (18). The very next sentence describes Havermeyer, "who liked peanut brittle . . . and shot tiny field mice every night with huge bullets from the .45 he had stolen from the dead man in Yossarian's tent" (18). Here "the dead man" comes as a mildly humorous shock; he will gain in meaning later.

Immediately afterward is mention of the tent "McWatt no longer shared with Clevinger" (18). The paragraph ends with "the officers' club that Yossarian had not helped build" (18), which is described in the paragraph following as "a splendid structure, and Yossarian throbbed with a mighty sense of accomplishment each time he gazed at it and reflected that none of the work that had gone into it was his" (19). The paragraph after that ends with a bald example of contradiction: we are told of Appleby that "everyone who knew him liked him," only to read in the next sentence, "'I hate that son of a bitch,' Yossarian growled" (19). The proper rejoinder to Yossarian's line does not come up for another page, when Clevinger notes that Appleby is not even there. In between is a long passage of echolalic dialogue, following upon Yossarian's flattening of a ping-pong ball:

> "That Yossarian," the two officers laughed, shaking their heads, and got another ball from the box on the shelf.
> "That Yossarian," Yossarian answered them.
> "Yossarian," Nately whispered cautioningly.
> "You see what I mean?" asked Clevinger.
> The officers laughed again when they heard Yossarian mimicking them. "That Yossarian," they said more loudly.
> "That Yossarian," Yossarian echoed.
> "Yossarian, please," Nately pleaded.
> "You see what I mean?" asked Clevinger. (19)

This exchange is followed by the resumption of Yossarian's argument with Clevinger, which is the framework for everything in the chapter and to which the narrative keeps returning between digressions. The speech of this argument is full of the rhetorical devices found in the narrative as a whole: echolalic repetitions, contradictions, deflations, misjoinders of subject and tone, and surprise transitions. The central issue is summed up in a few sentences in the chapter's first paragraph: "All over the world, boys on every side of the bomb line were laying down their lives for what they had been told was their country, and no one seemed to mind, least of all the boys who were laying down their young lives. There was no end in sight. The only end in sight was Yossarian's own. . ." (16). Not only do these lines deflate clichés and conventional attitudes, but they also deflate the issue of the war to a matter of Yossarian's personal survival.

Yossarian does as much over and over in the face of Clevinger's passionate conviction; every time Clevinger observes that Yossarian is not being singled out for destruction since *everyone's* life is endangered by the war, he answers, "And what difference does that make?" In other words, Yossarian is no *less* threatened simply because thousands of others are threatened as well. Of course, for anyone to express a paranoid fear that people are conspiring to kill him seems ludicrous in a wartime setting, and at this stage in the narrative Yossarian's in-spired cowardice is comic.

Even this early in the story Heller deftly hints, however, that the comedy may not be so funny after all. Part of Yossarian's "proof" is that "strangers he didn't know shot at him with cannons every time he flew up into the air to drop bombs on them, and it wasn't funny at all," and it isn't if one looks at that sentence's literal, albeit trivialized, description of warfare. "And if that wasn't funny," the paragraph goes on, "there were lots of things that weren't even funnier" (17). What follows offers the sort of grotesque disparity between subject and tone more characteristic of later sections of the novel, as it describes "the placid blue sea . . . that could gulp down a person with a cramp in the twinkling of an eye and ship him back to shore three days later, all charges paid, bloated, blue and putrescent, water draining out through both cold nostrils" (18).

Another device that turns up in chapter 2, and insistently throughout this first section, is the allegation of madness. During their argument Clevinger and Yossarian accuse each other of being crazy. In the paragraph describing Yossarian's fellow fliers, both McWatt and Nately are also called crazy. Earlier, during his conversation with the chaplain in chapter 1, Yossarian maintains that Nately is "loony" and warns the chaplain against the other wards on the grounds that they are "filled with lunatics" and "Insanity is contagious" (14). In chapters 3 and 4 we learn that Hungry Joe is crazy, though he thinks Yossarian is crazy. Also in chapter 4 Clevinger considers Dunbar crazy, Halfoat calls Daneeka crazy, Daneeka calls everyone crazy, Yossarian observes that Orr is crazy, and Havermeyer tells Appleby that he is crazy. Chapter 7 begins with the information that "McWatt was the craziest combat man of them all probably, because he was perfectly sane and still did not mind the war" (61). Looking ahead to the end of chapter 10, as the narrative moves into the Great Big Siege of Bologna, Dr. Stubbs says of Yossarian, who at the moment is refusing to fly that mission, "That crazy bastard may be the only sane one left" (114)—an instance of the device of madness combined with oxymoron.

Regarding another widely used rhetorical device, meaningless or paradoxical choices, the best examples in chapter 2 are those that Yossarian offers Clevinger in the course of their argument, such as:

> "Who, specifically, do you think is trying to murder you?"
> "Every one of them," Yossarian told him.
> "Every one of whom?"
> "Every one of whom do you think?" (17)

Better examples of this device come from elsewhere in this section. There is the practice of Gus and Wes, Doc Daneeka's orderlies, dealing with men who visit the medical tent by arbitrarily giving separate treatments for those with temperatures over or under 102, though they do not know what to do if the man's temperature is exactly 102. But the best example, and the most significant from the story's standpoint, is Catch-22 itself, as described in the oft-quoted scene between Yossarian and Daneeka in chapter 5:

There was only one catch and that was Catch-22, which specified that a concern for one's own safety in the face of dangers that were real and immediate was the process of a rational mind. Orr was crazy and could be grounded. All he had to do was ask; and as soon as he did, he would no longer be crazy and would have to fly more missions. Orr would be crazy to fly more missions and sane if he didn't, but if he was sane he had to fly them. If he flew them he was crazy and didn't have to; but if he didn't want to he was sane and had to. (47)

Even Catch-22 comes across as humorous at this point, and the narrative does not allow the reader to ponder it and its "spinning reasonableness" for long before it goes on to the flies in Appleby's eyes. Here, in the first section of the story, it simply joins the other contradictions and paradoxes characteristic of the general, and still mostly whimsical, madness.

One more stylistic device, used initially with humorous effect, merits attention: the confusion of words and meanings or even words and things. In practice this ranges from simple puns to the substitution of the signifier for the signified. A low-level example is Yossarian's censoring of letters in the hospital: instead of blacking them out on the basis of sense, as his task presumably dictates, he whimsically declares war on particular categories of words, first modifiers, then articles, and then every word in the letters but the salutations and signatures. Along similar lines is Wintergreen's participation in the war of memos between Generals Peckem and Dreedle, which Wintergreen decides in Dreedle's favor by throwing out Peckem's memos solely because he finds them "too prolix." Peckem begs such a response since he himself represents a triumph of style over substance.

An intentionally comic use of this confusion of words and meanings is the interplay from chapter 4 opened by Doc Daneeka:

"A little grease is what makes the world go round. One hand washes the other. Know what I mean? You scratch my back, I'll scratch yours."

Yossarian knew what he meant.

"That's not what I meant," Doc Daneeka said, as Yossarian
began scratching his back. (34)

This sort of word play is reminiscent of mainstream comedy, particularly as practiced in Heller's time by the Marx Brothers and S. J. Perelman. It is Perelman, for instance, who created lines such as "with a
blow I sent him grovelling. In ten minutes he was back with a basket
of appetising fresh-picked grovels"; and "Our meal finished, we saun-
tered into the rumpus room and Diana turned on the radio. With a
savage snarl the radio turned on her"[54]; and who could have also created the moment in the Marx Brothers' *Duck Soup* when Harpo, as a
spy, is asked for someone's record and pulls out a gramophone disk.
While little of Heller's word play exists at this playfully surreal
level, the "discontinuity" of the language, as Gary W. Davis terms this
severing of word and meaning, signifier and signified, functions prom-
inently in the novel, if in different forms.[55] When Yossarian moves the
bomb line on the map during the Great Big Siege of Bologna, for instance, and thereby convinces everyone that Bologna is captured, he
is substituting symbol for fact. In the same chapter he drunkenly in-
vents the rumor of a Lepage glue gun, only to be horrified moments
later when the rumor returns to him as truth. Words and names have
a tendency to take on life of their own in the world of *Catch-22,* at
first with comic results; the results grow less comic, however, as the
narrative moves into the later chapters.

In fact, all the rhetorical devices discussed so far, and specifically
the humorous ones, alter in significance as the book progresses. The
repetitions, contradictions, negations, deflations, and paradoxes become so commonplace by the end of the first nine chapters that they
lose the element of surprise and thus much of their risibleness. If they
were intended solely to be comic, the charge that the book's humor is
trivial and redundant would tend to hold. By the end of this opening
section of the novel, however, not only do the more insistent verbal
repetitions and contradictions, as well as the repeated allegations of
madness, taper off, they shift in function from mere stylistic devices to
motifs embedded in the entire foundation of the book's structure.

Repetition, for instance, shows up not only in the echolalic dialogue, but also in the recycling of certain scenes, such as Yossarian's arguments with Clevinger, his pleading with Doc Daneeka, Hungry Joe's nightmares, and the introductory mentions of Milo and Snowden, followed a chapter or so later in each case by expanded mentions. Other references to repetition—often by twos—and recurrent cycles appear in these chapters; these, in turn, point ahead to repetitions and cycles in the chapters to come, giving us the motif of déjà vu already acknowledged to be an important element of the novel's structure.

The soldier in white, for example, is always seen recycling the same two bottles. The scene concerning the original plastered soldier appears twice, in chapters 1 and 17. Chapter 18 features the soldier who sees everything twice. A second soldier in white shows up in chapter 34. Chapter 6 mentions the episode of Yossarian directing his plane twice over the bridge at Ferrara, which is offered up again in chapter 13; there it spawns an argument between Yossarian and Colonels Cathcart and Korn over how the problem can be handled, which itself goes around twice. Yossarian's squadron is the 256th—"two to the fighting eighth power," as he tells the chaplain in chapter 1. And, although an afterthought born of necessity, the number of the famous catch, and thus the title of the novel, also contains two twos.

Many of the characters also appear in doubles or pairs; in the early chapters Appleby and Havermeyer are linked by their similar attitudes, as are Clevinger and Nately, and Yossarian and Dunbar. In the first section Colonel Cathcart is all but inseparable from Colonel Korn; General Peckem is linked to General Dreedle; Doc Daneeka is contrasted with Doctor Stubbs. Some characters *only* appear in pairs: operations officers Piltchard and Wren, medical orderlies Gus and Wes.

As the repetition of language suggests the repetitive structure, so do the other rhetorical devices of the first section—oxymoron, deflation, paradox, insanity, linguistic discontinuity—suggest larger structural and thematic motifs. Together they create the general atmosphere of insanity and absurdity that sets the tone and internal (il)logic of the Catch-22 cosmos. Individually these motifs rise to their full significance in the later sections of the novel and will thus be discussed later.

But one can already see the transformation from stylistic device to thematic motif by the climax of this first section in the chapters containing those two aforementioned set pieces, Clevinger's trial and the history of Major Major Major. These episodes therefore merit closer reading.

CLEVINGER'S TRIAL AND MAJOR MAJOR

Howard J. Stark places a positive light on one complaint of some critics when he observes that although chapters 8 and 9 interrupt the flow of the narrative, they do function by "repeating, in essence, the ideas and images of the first seven chapters, *déjà vu,* just presenting them in another way."[56] For Brian Way, the novel does not get earnest until the episode of Clevinger's court-martial, which marks the point where the humor of the first seventy pages is "transformed into a weapon."[57]

Chapter 8 ("Lieutenant Scheisskopf") begins, as so many of these chapters do, with a bridge from the previous chapter, which ends with the question of how Milo could buy eggs for seven cents in Malta and make a profit while selling them for five. "Not even Clevinger understood how Milo could do that," the new chapter opens, "and Clevinger knew everything" (69). Following a recap of Yossarian's arguments with Clevinger about the war, the narrative goes on to a capsule description of Clevinger, a frequent characterization technique of the novel that helps keep the personages flat but brightly colored, like the satirical caricatures they are. Clevinger, we are told, is a bright intellectual with a developed social conscience, a Harvard-trained liberal idealist. He has, in a typical oxymoron, "lots of intelligence and no brains. . . . In short, he was a dope" (70). This conclusion is followed up a paragraph later by the equally oxymoronic "He was a very serious, very earnest, and very conscientious dope," and after a few one-sentence jibes intended to demonstrate as much, the narrative finishes this description with "Yossarian tried to help him. 'Don't be a dope,' he had counseled. . ." (70).

Suddenly, the narrative jumps back to cadet school in Santa Ana, where Yossarian is advising Clevinger not to tell Scheisskopf why cadet morale is poor, even though Scheisskopf is begging to know. Clevinger the helpful idealist, a believer in reason and language, takes him at his word; Yossarian, who seems to know this world better, insists that Scheisskopf is divorcing word and meaning, saying the opposite of what he appears to be saying:

> "He *wants* someone to tell him," Clevinger said.
> "He wants everyone to keep still, idiot," Yossarian answered.
> "Didn't you hear him?" Clevinger argued.
> "I heard him," Yossarian replied. "I heard him say very loudly and very distinctly that he wants every one of us to keep our mouths shut if we know what's good for us." (71)

After a description of the asinine Lieutenant Scheisskopf and his monomaniacal obsession with parades, with internal digressions to his loose wife and her looser friend Dori Duz, the narrative finally circles back to the outcome of Clevinger's idealistic response to Lieutenant Scheisskopf. It does so in a typical long sentence with an internal transition produced by mismatched clauses: "Actually, no one but Lieutenant Scheisskopf really gave a damn about the parades, least of all the bloated colonel with the big fat mustache, who was chairman of the Action Board and began bellowing at Clevinger the moment Clevinger stepped gingerly into the room to plead innocent to the charges Lieutenant Scheisskopf had lodged against him" (76).

Clevinger finds himself confronting not only Scheisskopf—who, we are informed in an echolalic paragraph, is at once his prosecutor, defense officer, and judge—but also one Major Metcalf and the "bloated colonel with the big fat mustache" who takes charge of the interrogation. Throughout the five-page scene, the colonel bullies not only Clevinger but everyone else in the room. The dialogue is characterized by much repetition:

> "Will you speak up, please? I couldn't hear you."
> "Yes, sir. I—"

"Will you speak up, please? He couldn't hear you."
"Yes, sir. I—"
"Metcalf."
"Sir?"
"Didn't I tell you to keep your stupid mouth shut?"
"Yes, sir."
"Then keep your stupid mouth shut when I tell you to keep
your stupid mouth shut. Do you understand? Will you speak up,
please? I couldn't hear you."

The repetition reaches its absurd peak when the corporal who is re-
cording the proceedings repeats back to the colonel his own repetition
of the colonel:

"Read me back the last line."
"'Read me back the last line,'" read back the corporal, who
could take shorthand.
"Not *my* last line, stupid!" the colonel shouted.
"Somebody else's."
"'Read me back the last line,'" read back the corporal.
"That's *my* last line again!" shrieked the colonel, turning pur-
ple with anger.
"Oh, no, sir," corrected the corporal. "That's *my* last line. I
read it to you just a moment ago." (80–81)

Critics have compared these exchanges to the Marx Brothers and the
Abbott and Costello of "Who's on first." Another example from S. J.
Perelman shows just how much Heller's rhetoric here borrows from
the humorists of the 1930s:

"Just a minute," rapped the manager, wheeling on him.
"Are you trying to take sides with the clientele?"
"No, no, of course not," stammered Rightwich, overcome
with confusion. "All I mean is—"
"We've got an ugly name for that in our business, boy." Left-
wich's eyes had narrowed to mere slits. "It's called taking sides with
the clientele."[58]

Like so many figures of authority in *Catch-22*, the colonel with the big fat mustache blithely indulges in direct self-contradiction, as when he tells Clevinger, "We're not at all interested in what you did say to Yossarian," only to add a second later, "What did you say to Yossarian?" (82) More comic and to the point are the tortured negations into which Clevinger is forced by his interrogators. Metcalf, for instance, orders Clevinger to say "sir" when he doesn't interrupt. And while the colonel shuts Metcalf up for not making sense, he backs Clevinger into the statements, "I always didn't say you couldn't punish me, sir" (79), and "I always didn't say you couldn't find me guilty, sir" (82). Such forced verbal distortions are noteworthy because they show, for all their comic effect, how authority can set the parameters of discourse, so that words are sundered from their meanings, and language from reason. As George Orwell, one of the subliminal influences on Heller's novel, observed in *1984* and elsewhere, if authority can control language, it can control thought.

Ultimately, nothing Clevinger says makes any difference anyway, since his guilt has already been determined before the hearing: "Clevinger was guilty, of course, or he would not have been accused, and since the only way to prove it was to find him guilty, it was their patriotic duty to do so" (82). The reasoning here, of course, contains the usual circular and inverted syllogism: Clevinger's guilt does not follow from proving the charges; the charges are proof of Clevinger's guilt.

In a not uncommon practice, Heller makes the moral of this episode clear in the final page of the chapter. As authority figures, the members of the Action Board hate Clevinger and his fellow inferiors with a "brutal, uncloaked, inexorable hatred." Nowhere among the enemy "were there men who hated him more" (83). Nothing so far has confirmed more baldly Yossarian's argument that the battle in *Catch-22* is not between the Allies and the Axis, but between the powerless and the powerful, the victims and the victimizers. Unfortunately, the powerful are in the position to set the standards for the battle, even the standards of discourse. It is a sober conclusion to a very funny scene.

Immediately on the heels of this scene comes the chapter that features Major Major Major Major, whose very name begs the matter of repetition. He also embodies in his person the verbal motifs that have haunted this section: the contradictions, negations, and deflated clichés. "Some men are born mediocre, some men achieve mediocrity, and some men have mediocrity thrust upon them. With Major Major it had been all three. Even among men lacking all distinction he inevitably stood out as a man lacking more distinction than all the rest, and people who met him were always impressed by how unimpressive he was" (85).

The rest of the chapter maintains this tone, through the long, digressive description of Major Major's insufferable father, a farmer of Calvinist background, presumably the salt of American earth, who is "a God-fearing, freedom-loving, law-abiding rugged individualist who held that federal aid to anyone but farmers was creeping socialism. He advocated thrift and hard work and disapproved of loose women who turned him down. His specialty was growing alfalfa, and he made a good thing out of not growing any" (85). The remainder of the description casts Major Major's father as the ultimate hypocrite, preaching traditional American values and applying none of them to himself. He is also possessed of a cruel sense of humor, equalled only by that of Major Major's nemesis Captain Black, a sense of humor that allows him to take advantage of his labor-ravaged wife and give his newborn son the name Major Major Major and to pretend otherwise until the boy enters school, and to greet with indifference that shock, which kills his wife and permanently destroys Major Major by giving him a major identity crisis that lasts his lifetime. True to the discontinuity of signifier and signified, Major Major is dominated by his name, the fact that he "was some total stranger named Major Major Major about whom he knew nothing" and who other children spurn for "pretending to be someone they had known for years" (87).

His father is only the first of many forces that victimize Major Major, a quintessential victim. He takes seriously all the clichés of proper behavior preached, but not practiced by his traditional Calvinist-American milieu; he rigorously obeys the Ten Commandments and all other conventional attitudes, "he always looked before he leaped. . . . He turned the other cheek on every occasion and always did unto others exactly as he would have had others do unto him" (87). For his wholehearted obedience to the social prescriptions of his elders, he is of course disliked by them as "a flagrant nonconformist" (88).

It is the doom of the hapless Major Major Major to remain obediently at the mercy of forces wholly beyond his control. He continues to be bullied and generally disliked, and even his serendipitous promotions—from private to major overnight by the whim of an IBM machine, to squadron commander by the whim of Colonel Cathcart—have no rational connection with his merits or desires and turn out to be disasters. Unlike Clevinger, Major Major finally comes to understand the illogical rules of this world: he gives Sergeant Towser the oxymoronic instructions about letting people in to see him only when he is out, and contradicts himself in the very last scene of the chapter when, after being tackled by Yossarian, he reminds himself that he absolutely cannot tell Yossarian there is nothing he can do, only to say, "there's nothing I can do" (107).

Coming so soon after the confrontation of the idealistic Clevinger with his brutal inquisitors, the story of Major Major underlines the contradictions inherent in the practice and the preachment of our traditional ideals. The issue will come into greater prominence later, in the detailing of the character of Chaplain Tappman, who more than anyone else in the novel is victimized for his adherence to traditional values, and shares characteristics with both Clevinger and Major Major.

Major Major turns out to be a catalyst of sorts. The motifs of repetition, contradiction, and deflation of clichés and ideals that have characterized the rhetorical style of the narrative thus far are made flesh in his character. From this chapter on these devices are not quite so insistent in the prose. They are still present, however, in a more fundamental form, functioning as the underlying rules of the cosmos—read "chaos"—of the novel.

6

Bologna: Death, Injustice, and Absurdity

Chapter 10, and thus the second division of the novel, begins with the statement: "Clevinger was dead. That was the basic flaw in his philosophy" (107). Clevinger's death, it should be recalled, immediately precedes Yossarian's flight to the hospital with forty-four missions, which sets up the first chapter. Its mention at the beginning of the Great Big Siege of Bologna thus brings the novel circling back to its opening and closes off the first section. This is the first death of a character with whom the reader has become involved.

Two other deaths of underlying importance are also returned to in this chapter: Kraft's and Mudd's. Kraft's death is a source of guilt for Yossarian, since Kraft was killed when Yossarian flew a second time over the bridge at Ferrara in order to avoid having to do the whole mission over. Mudd is the dead man in Yossarian's tent, although here it is explained that what Yossarian refers to as the dead man in his tent is really the belongings of a man who was sent on a mission and killed before he could officially report for duty. Since he was not, on paper, part of the squadron yet, his death in combat could not formally have taken place: "Because he had never officially gotten into the squadron, he could never officially be gotten out . . ." (111).

Dehumanization

49

Mudd is one character who represents all those soldiers who die in war, and particularly the unknown soldiers, we are told here, who by definition must be dead. Though he has a name, even that name suggests the return of human life to inorganic components, and under his more usual cognomen "the dead man" he is as good as anonymous.

Amid these deaths comes the announcement that Colonel Cathcart has volunteered the group for Bologna. Though death has naturally been an issue in the whimsical first section of the novel—escaping it is Yossarian's rationale for being in the hospital when we first see him, and the ethic of staying alive is behind most of Yossarian's arguments with Clevinger—death takes on a new seriousness now.

> The clinging, overpowering conviction of death spread steadily with the continuing rainfall, soaking mordantly into each man's ailing countenance like the corrosive blot of some crawling disease. Everyone smelled of formaldehyde. There was nowhere to turn for help, not even to the medical tent, which had been ordered closed by Colonel Korn so that no one could report for sick call. . . . With sick call suspended and the door to the medical tent nailed shut, Doc Daneeka spent the intervals between rain perched on a high stool, wordlessly absorbing the bleak outbreak of fear with a sorrowing neutrality, roosting like a melancholy buzzard below the ominous, hand-lettered sign tacked up on the closed door of the medical tent by Captain Black as a joke and left hanging there by Doc Daneeka because it was no joke. The sign was bordered in dark crayon and read: "CLOSED UNTIL FURTHER NOTICE. DEATH IN THE FAMILY." (112)

Surrounding this announcement are a number of short and loosely connected digressions: Wintergreen at Lowery Field, reference to Milo's bombing of the squadron, the Splendid Atabrine Insurrection and Appleby's subsequent humiliation at Major Major's tent. Over the course of the Great Big Siege of Bologna there will be other digressions that take up entire chapters. The first of them, coming with chapter 11 before the Bologna campaign gets going in earnest, is another of those set pieces that stands out from the general chaos of the narrative: the Glorious Loyalty Oath Crusade of the sadistic Captain Black.

Captain Black's Glorious Loyalty Oath Crusade has been singled out as an interruption, albeit droll, a tangential excursion, like Clevinger's trial or Major Major's history, that sidetracks the narrative. It is in fact connected to the two earlier episodes, not just because the Crusade is directed at Major Major for winning the squadron commander's post that Captain Black coveted, but because it dramatizes once again the nature of power in the world of Catch-22.

It should be noted that all three digressions reflect to some extent Heller's loathing of the Joseph McCarthy legacy. McCarthy was the notorious senator from Wisconsin who chaired the congressional hearings of the House Un-American Activities Committee in the years surrounding the Korean War. He epitomized the rabid anticommunism of the early cold war period, finding communists, ex-communists, and communist sympathizers everywhere throughout American life. There was no escape from the depredations of McCarthyism; people called up to testify before HUAC had no constitutional guarantees to protect them. If they refused to give McCarthy the information he wanted, even when pleading the Fifth Amendment right that protects against self-incrimination, they could be summarily imprisoned for contempt of Congress. Sometimes even being called as an unfriendly witness was enough to prove one's guilt (if you were not guilty, why would you have been called?), and many who managed to avoid imprisonment found themselves blacklisted, which usually meant they lost their livelihoods and most of their friends and associates, who could also be blacklisted simply for having ties to them.

Among those who suffered were writers (Dashiell Hammett, Howard Fast, Dalton Trumbo), government bureaucrats (Alger Hiss), and even Robert Oppenheimer, the physicist who had headed the Manhattan Project that gave the United States the atomic bomb. A few benefited, such as Congressman Richard Nixon, who opened and shut the case against Alger Hiss by providing evidence found in a pumpkin, and Actor's Guild president Ronald Reagan, who was called before HUAC as a friendly witness and got rid of his political opposition in Hollywood by "naming names." During this era loyalty oaths proliferated; it was difficult, if not impossible, to gain employment in the public or private sector without signing one. Politicians, Democrat and Republican alike, fell over one another in public trying to prove who was more patriotic by proposing tougher and tougher legislation against the leftist threat.

It was not until McCarthy began looking for communists in the U.S. Army that the newly elected President Eisenhower took action by throwing the hearings on television, then a young medium, and giving McCarthy enough airtime to hang himself. McCarthy eventually died a broken man in an alcoholic ward of a sanatorium, but his legacy lasted. Of the friendlies who became presidents of the United States nothing need be said. Less known is that in some states it is still obligatory to sign a loyalty oath before gaining employment in the public sector (I know from personal experience that as recently as 1984 a notarized loyalty oath was required by the University of California.).

If the Glorious Loyalty Oath Crusade is clearly satirizing contemporary history, it also serves to reinforce one of the cornerstones of this fictive world's foundation, summed up in the remark that "the combat men in the squadron found themselves dominated by the administrators appointed to serve them" (117). Such is the case with Mudd, not only killed but obliterated from any kind of existence by the likes of Captains Piltchard and Wren and Sergeant Towser. In the "Bologna" chapter General Peckem reappears, a consummate administrator who serves the troops as commander of Special Services, and who will stop at nothing to increase his power over the men; it is here that the narrative tells us that Peckem believes "that all combat units in the theater should be placed under the jurisdiction of the Special Service Corps," since "[i]f dropping bombs on the enemy was not a special service . . . what in the world was" (124). Linked once more to Peckem is the lowly ex-P.F.C. Wintergreen, with his power as ruler of the mailroom here extending into the international black market.

At every level, the exercise of power leads to injustice. Black completely alters the operation of the squadron during his crusade, and the campaign created to victimize the easily victimized Major Major soon victimizes everyone. Black also relishes seeing the men sent off to death over Bologna. The other administrators, from Peckem down to Wintergreen, insist that it is the duty of the men to risk their lives in combat while they carefully remain aloof from danger themselves. As Wintergreen tells Yossarian, "If I'm destined to unload these lighters at a profit and pick up some Egyptian cotton cheap from Milo, then that's what I'm going to do. And if you're destined to be killed over Bologna, then you're going to be killed, so you might just as well go out and die like a man" (126). On the very next page Clevinger endorses this view by insisting to Yossarian, albeit uncertainly, that it is Colonel Cathcart's business, not Yossarian's, whether or not Yossarian gets killed. Clevinger has bought the terms of the system, despite his own victimization at its hands.

Yossarian fights back vigorously, however, to save his life. During the course of the Bologna campaign he wins a few temporary battles against the system by using its own mad terms against it. Buying the importance of the bomb line on the map, he moves it and gets the missions canceled for a time. He has Corporal Snark poison the men with laundry soap again. When he finds himself at last in the air, he sabotages his intercom, providing an excuse to turn back.

The narrative of Yossarian's guerrilla war for survival during the Great Big Siege of Bologna is interrupted by chapter 13, which digresses to Major —— de Coverley to detail his acquisition of apartments in Rome for the men (needed as background for the "Luciana" chapter soon to follow) and his promotion of Milo to mess officer. The rest of the chapter returns to Ferrara to describe in more detail Yossarian's circular bombing of the bridge, Kraft's death, and Yossarian's circular exchange with Cathcart and Korn concerning giving him a medal for the mission. This deal struck between Yossarian and Korn foreshadows the more odious deal at the book's end.

Finally, despite all his actions during the Great Big Siege of Bologna, Yossarian ends up over the target, surrounded by flak, screaming evasive commands at his pilot McWatt. His whole process of struggling against the apparently inevitable is made flesh in his scene with Aarfy, who calmly blocks the escape crawlway while sudden death threatens the plane. Yossarian screams at him, but Aarfy does not hear; Yossarian punches him in the stomach to make him move, but Aarfy does not feel: "There was no resistance, no response at all from the soft, insensitive mass, and after a while Yossarian's spirit died. . . . He was overcome with a humiliating feeling of impotence. . ." (153). Nevertheless, Yossarian does not give up and bodily drags Aarfy back into the fuselage, only to find it has become a den of snow; flak ripping through a stack of maps has filled the space with paper fragments. Even this icy brush with death leaves the moronically brutish Aarfy in a "state of rapturous contentment" (154).

Coming at the climax of chapter 15 and the Bologna campaign, this scene contains the most dramatic description of air battle in the entire book:

> Behind him, men were dying. Strung out for miles in a stricken, tortuous, squirming line, the other flights of planes were making the same hazardous journey over the target, threading their swift way through the swollen masses of new and old bursts of flak like rats racing in a pack through their own droppings. One was on fire, and flapped lamely off by itself, billowing gigantically like a monstrous blood-red star. As Yossarian watched, the burning plane floated over on its side and began spiraling down slowly in wide, tremulous, narrowing circles, its huge flaming burden blazing orange and flaring out in back like a long, swirling cape of fire and smoke. There were parachutes, one, two, three . . . four, and then the plane gyrated into a spin and fell the rest of the way to the ground, fluttering insensibly inside its vivid pyre like a shred of colored tissue paper. One whole flight of planes from another squadron had been blasted apart. (154–155)

There is nothing funny about this paragraph—none of the customary wisecracks or other deflations, and only a few similes suggesting the misjoinder of subject and tone. Death is serious business here.

Following this climactic battle over Bologna, the narrative relents and digresses once again, this time to one of the few islands of calm in the book, Yossarian's encounter with Luciana. Heller included this episode, according to his *Playboy* interview, because something similar actually happened to him, even including his throwing the woman's address away afterward. True to the world of *Catch-22*, however, Yossarian's dialogue with Luciana contains many oxymoronic syllogisms: he doesn't want to dance or dine with her, but he does want to sleep with her; Luciana will not marry him because he is crazy because he wants to marry her. In context it stands as a perfect moment in support of love and life; but as a perfect moment it cannot be sustained in the imperfect world of the novel.

The imperfections of this world of death and injustice are extensively outlined in the two chapters that finish off this section. These chapters take place predominantly in hospitals, where Death, Yossarian notes, is a much more orderly business than it is outside the hospital.

> They couldn't dominate Death inside the hospital, but they certainly made her behave. . . . There was none of that crude, ugly ostentation about dying that was so common outside the hospital. They did not blow up in mid-air like Kraft or the dead man in Yossarian's tent, or freeze to death in the blazing summertime the way Snowden had frozen to death after spilling his secret to Yossarian in the back of the plane. . . . They didn't take it on the lam weirdly inside a cloud the way Clevinger had done. They didn't explode into blood and clotted matter. They didn't drown or get struck by lightning, mangled by machinery or crushed in landslides. They didn't get shot to death in hold-ups, strangled to death in rapes, stabbed to death in saloons, bludgeoned to death with axes by parents or children, or die summarily by some other act of God. (170)

And this litany of death goes on for the remainder of a long paragraph.

In chapter 17 the soldier in white reappears along with the Texan, and we have circled back to the scene of chapter 1. This time, however, the meaning of the soldier in white seems less comic and more sinister; coming after so many scenes of death and destruction, he is now "the bright reminder" of a "nauseating truth," to wit, the anonymity of pain and death and the indifference of the cosmos. Yossarian decides that Nurse Cramer is eventually responsible for killing him, since she is the one who reads the thermometer and detects his death—another case of the inversion of cause and effect, of signifier and signified.

Watching the nurses switch the bottles of liquid around the soldier in white prompts the men in the ward to a discussion of universal justice. They compare maladies, unable to account for any of them within a reasonable system of rewards and punishments. Near the end of the discussion a warrant officer concludes, "Just for once I'd like to see all these things sort of straightened out, with each person getting exactly what he deserves. It might give me some confidence in this universe" (175).

A page later Yossarian is contemplating all the possible things that could do him in, in a page-long list that begins with Hitler and Mussolini and ends with Ewing's tumor and melanoma. He longs to spend all his life in the hospital surrounded by a battery of doctors, and fears "the first chill, flush, twinge, ache, belch, sneeze, stain, lethargy, vocal slip, loss of balance or lapse of memory that would signal the inevitable beginning of the inevitable end" (178).

Continuing the hospital motif, chapter 18 jumps back to Yossarian's first experiences as a malingerer while still in training at Lowery Field and Santa Ana. Following Yossarian's initiation into the quiet pleasures of the hospital and the introduction of the soldier who sees everything twice comes his discussion with Scheisskopf's wife about God. Though both agree they are atheists, the Gods they do not believe in are very different. Yossarian accuses God of bungling the universe. "Good God," he says, with pointed irony on the narrator's part, "how much reverence can you have for a Supreme Being who finds it necessary to include such phenomena as phlegm and tooth decay in His divine system of creation? What in the world was running through that warped, evil, scatological mind of His when He robbed old people of the power to control their bowel movements? Why in the world did He ever create pain?" (184).

Scheisskopf's wife tearfully and contradictorily insists that the God she does not believe in is a good, just, merciful God. Yossarian's God, however, is the one that seems to run the world of the novel. In these discussions that dominate the climactic chapters of the Bologna section, He presides over the multiple injustices of a universe in which rewards and punishments are distributed at apparent random, in which human life is constantly jeopardized by an assortment of dangers, accidents, and diseases, and in which death, the ultimate return of humanity and flesh to inorganic components, is the worst injustice of all.

A morbidly humorous coda to this dialectic of death and injustice appears at the end of the section when Yossarian is persuaded to take the place of the dead soldier who saw everything twice in order to give the dead soldier's family someone to visit. For the doctor, "one dying boy is just as good as any other," since to the rational, scientific mind "all dying boys are equal" (187). The visiting mother echoes this notion, and Yossarian's earlier rejoinders to Clevinger, when in replying to the question of whether Yossarian is Yossarian or her son Giuseppe she says, "What difference does it make? . . . He's dying" (190–191). As both Yossarian and Dunbar have noted thus far, this is true for everyone; everyone's life is slipping inexorably away, and far more rapidly for those in combat. The cosmic injustice of this fact and the question of God's competence return in the last exchange of the chapter, when Giuseppe's brother urges the renamed Yossarian to tell God "it ain't right for people to die when they're young. . . . Tell Him if they got to die at all, they got to die when they're old. . . . I don't think He knows it ain't right, because he's supposed to be good and it's been going on for a long, long time" (191).

As noted earlier, many critics have viewed these two hospital chapters, taken together, as a major turning point in the novel. The insistent rhetorical devices of the first section have pretty much disappeared from the prose: what was stylistic has become structural; what was comic in the early parts of the novel has taken on a darker hue. The dialectic on God, death, and cosmic injustice that fills these chapters raises the level of the discourse from the merely satirical to the philosophical. From here on, as Jesse Ritter phrases it, "The absurd gives way to the Absurd."[59]

Exactly what does that statement mean? And is it true?

ABSURDITY AND THE ABSURD

In its most general sense, the literature of the absurd is that which diverges in form and content from the realistic or "mimetic" tradition, widely regarded as dominant in our age of reason. Fictions and plays in the absurd mode tend to turn natural law and probability on its head, or at least stretch it severely, usually with surreal, grotesque, and satirical results. Students of the absurd sometimes point to fantastic satires such as Rabelais's *Pantagruel*, Swift's *Gulliver's Travels*, and Lewis Carroll's Alice books as forerunners of the modern absurd. More in a direct line is the work of nineteenth century Russian Nikolay Gogol, who in *The Government Inspector* and *Dead Souls* burlesqued the pretentions of czarist Russia and in *The Nose* told an absurd tale of a man whose nose, cut off at the barber's, takes on a life of its own (an image Woody Allen borrowed for the climax of his farce *Sleeper*). The absurd, in this sense, makes free use of exaggerations, surreal circumstances, and a grotesque and frequently unpleasant humor, usually recognizably connected, albeit in skewed fashion, to mimetic reality. Max F. Schulz, discussing one recent aspect of the absurd, black humor, captures the sense of the whole form when he states that the aesthetic enjoyment of it derives in large part "from the aptness of its fictional worlds, from the deftness with which these fictional microcosms mirror the profound disjunctions of . . . life."[60]

The figure who most shaped the absurd literary tradition in the twentieth century was the Prague-based, German-speaking Jewish author Franz Kafka. Kafka claimed that in his fiction, parables, and aphorisms—indeed, in his neurotic person—he represented the negative tendencies of his age, a century that was beginning to suspect that all the faith that had been placed in reason and humanity in the century before was misplaced. History appears to have borne him out. His best-known works include *The Metamorphosis,* a story about a small-time traveling salesman who awakes one morning transformed into a giant insect, and the unfinished novels *The Trial* and *The Castle.*

In all of these, the hapless protagonists—respectively Gregor Samsa, Josef K., and K.—find themselves up against insurmountable and incomprehensible odds. Samsa, as an insect with the mind of a rational man, struggles, despite his condition, to go to work, dine with his family, and behave as though nothing is seriously wrong, but ultimately fails for reasons that are obvious; his reason is helpless to deal with his irrational circumstances. Josef K. of *The Trial* is arrested on the first page of the novel for an unspecified crime and spends the rest of the novel trying to clear himself without ever asking what the crime is. He works his way through the labyrinth of an impossible bureaucracy, compounding error with error, until he is exonerated, after which a pair of executioners turn up at his door and slit his throat. K. of *The Castle* is following up an alleged invitation for employment under the powerful though hopelessly confused bureaucracy of the Castle, but finds himself trapped in the labyrinth not only of that bureaucracy but of the village surrounding it, so that he never reaches his goal.

In the wake of these works and others, most of which were only published after Kafka's early death from tuberculosis, the adjective "Kafkaesque" has come to be applied to any situation in which the individual is up against overwhelming complexities and absurdities, usually institutional/bureaucratic in origin; the term has since been applied to fictions as different as *1984* and *Catch-22*, and to many situations in real life. One could only describe as "Kafkaesque," for instance, the suit filed against Franz Kafka by the IRS in 1987 for unpaid taxes on royalties; it was quickly and quietly withdrawn when the Service learned that not only was he not an American citizen, he had died in 1924.

Historically oriented critics have viewed Kafka's novels about individuals vying with irrational institutions as criticisms of the overloaded bureaucracy of the tottering Austro-Hungarian Empire, which Kafka himself served as a petty bureaucrat, and thus as a metaphor for all human systems of justice and acceptance, with their all-too-human abuses of power. More metaphysical critics, taking their cues from Kafka's friend and literary executor Max Brod, have sought Kafka's themes in his philosophical reading, particularly the work of the proto-existentialist thinker of nineteenth-century Denmark, Søren Kierkegaard.

Kierkegaard held, in the face of such dialectical materialists of his time as Hegel, that one could not reason one's way to the Absolute Truth. In his treatise *Fear and Trembling*, for instance, he uses the biblical story of Abraham and Isaac, in which God orders Abraham to sacrifice his only son to Him as proof of his faith and obedience. Abraham overcomes his fatherly feelings, ties his son onto the sacrificial altar, and raises the knife, only to have his hand stayed by God at the last moment. By humane, rational standards, neither Abraham nor God comes across particularly well in this tale. Kierkegaard observes, however, that one cannot apply such standards to God, who by definition rises above human judgment. One takes Him solely on faith, not through logic and reason, which are purely human systems through which He is inaccessible. Kierkegaard advocated an abandonment of reason and a "leap of faith" for apprehending the Absolute.

Those critics who have embraced the Kierkegaardian interpretation of Kafka have viewed the bureaucracies of *The Trial* and *The Castle* as Absolute in the divine sense and not to be questioned. Josef K. of *The Trial* is therefore, by definition, guilty; he proves his guilt by showing his willingness to accept the rules of the system, and to go through the court bureaucracies to dispute his arrest, and by never inquiring after the nature of his crime. But even if he is guilty, he is still, for commentator Helen Weinberg, a victim-hero, "a reasonable man, condemned to die in an absurd world."[61] Weinberg takes a position much more tenable than that of the strict Kierkegaardians, to wit, that, considering the fallibility of the bureaucracies in the novels, these institutions represent a human, pseudorational attempt to embody the absolute concepts of justice, order, and grace and are thus only "the world's meretricious embodiments of the mystery of the Law."[62]

This likelihood inheres in the parable to which Weinberg alludes, a parable told to Josef K. in *The Trial* by a priest; Kafka published it separately as "Vor dem Gesetz," which is translatable either as "Before the Court" or "Before the Law." In this anecdote a man approaches a gate manned by a sturdy gatekeeper, a gate presumably to the court of divine law and justice. The man is forbidden entry, however. The gatekeeper is too powerful to be overcome physically, and he is only the first of many that the man must pass. The man wastes his entire life arguing and pleading to persuade the gatekeeper to let him in.

Ultimately, on the brink of death, he learns that this gate was for him and him alone, just before the gatekeeper closes it against him. The Law is a mystery, not to be reached through conventional human means, not through reason or through that burlesque of reason—human institutions supposedly erected to serve the Law.

If God in Kafka is arbitrary and incomprehensible, an Absolute whose judgments cannot be understood let alone questioned, then human systems attempting to embody divine absolutes are if anything fallible but equally arbitrary gatekeepers standing between the individual and the Absolute. If one cannot even master the human dimensions of, say, justice, through human systems of logic and order, one certainly cannot apprehend the Divine in that way.

Kafka's most important contributions to the literary absurd, then, besides the dark slapstick of his tales, are his maddeningly complex human institutions—a grand metaphor for the inefficacy of rational structures—and a cosmos indifferently ruled by a God who is so remote as to be unreachable and even irrelevant for the common man. For the European Jews of the terrible period leading up to World War II, this Kafkaesque God was *der Gott, der sich entfernt hat* (the God who has distanced himself).

In the U.S., many of the best practitioners of the absurd have had, like Kafka, Jewish roots; critics have attempted to account for this tendency by looking at everything from the gloomy whimsy of the traditional Yiddish tale, embodied in the work of Sholom Aleichem, to the forced alienation of the Jew in the western world, exemplified most horrendously in the Nazi Holocaust. In the 1930s, Jewish-Americans gave us the absurd at its most whimsical in the films of the Marx Brothers, aided and abetted by New York-based humorists like George S. Kaufman and S. J. Perelman. In the same decade the darker side of the absurd was addressed by Perelman's close friend and brother-in-law Nathanael West, who, more than any other American of the time, was the heir to Kafka.

Nathanael West was reading Kafka in 1930 as he worked on his second novel *Miss Lonelyhearts*. Of his four novels, this one focuses most on the remoteness of God and the cruelty of the cosmos. Its protagonist, a male journalist who writes the advice column of a newspaper run by a cynical editor, finds himself unable to handle the agonies and injustices he confronts in the letters sent to him. He not only begins to question the justice of the universe, but also wonders if God is paying attention or if He even exists. As his doubts turn to self-delusion, Miss Lonelyhearts begins to take on the role of Christ himself and brings on an ironic martyrdom.

West's next novel, *A Cool Million,* was dedicated to S. J. Perelman. Of all his fiction it is the most comic, as Perelman noted, though the comedy is grotesque and harshly satirical. Its hero, the idealistic Lemuel Pitkin, sets out to seek his fortune in America, Horatio Alger–style, and ends up—like his predecessors Candide, Lemuel Gulliver, and Karl Rossman, the hapless innocent of Kafka's *Amerika*—the passive victim of one bizarre episode after another. Pitkin blithely holds on to his American dream of success through incredible depredations at the hands of con men, fascists, communists, tomahawk-wielding Indians, and sadistic vaudeville comics. Over the course of his adventures he is "dismantled," losing eye, limb, teeth, scalp, and finally his life, but never his stupid innocence, even when he is sold into white slavery.

In one of the few positive reviews this novel received upon its publication in 1934, critic John Chamberlain claimed that while reading it one must "either laugh . . . or go mad because of the insane reality that lies behind it. . . . There is . . . no genial, all-dissolving laughter in Mr. West. . . . His . . . satire is wry, piercing, painful. . . . [His] humor is a way of getting revenge for the indignities which one suffers. . . ."[63] His comments could just as well apply to Heller and *Catch-22.*

In fact, West is considered a pivotal figure in the development of American black humor, which came to dominate the literary absurd in the United States in the 1960s; in this sub-genre critics have placed not only Heller but Vladimir Nabokov, Kurt Vonnegut, Bruce Jay Friedman (who used the term himself), John Barth, and Stanley Elkin, among others. As an heir of the absurd, black humor aims its dark laughter at the apparent meaninglessness of the universe and the pathetic place of the individual therein. When God appears at all in works of modern black humor, he comes across poorly. In Bruce Jay Friedman's play *Steambath*, for instance, the afterlife is a public steambath, where God, posing as a Puerto Rican attendant, places the dead to amuse himself; when individuals begin to bore him, he sends them on to the void. In Stanley Elkin's novel *The Living End*, eternal punishments and rewards are distributed whimsically; God sends one perfectly decent man to a fire-and-brimstone hell, for example, because he kept his business open on Sunday and thought heaven looked like a theme park.

In his book *Black Humor Fiction of the Sixties*, Max F. Schulz notes that black humor is skeptical if not cynical, emphasizing with its little people caught in circumstances hysterically and grotesquely beyond their control "the bewildering trackless choices that face the individual" in the modern world.[64] For him, as for Robert Scholes, Céline's *Journey to the End of the Night* is the real progenitor of black humor, because of its "intensification of everyday troubles into an ironic vision of a distorted cosmos, where a poetic injustice reigns, which destroys all who do not learn to accommodate themselves to it."[65]

Schulz insists that the difference between the literary absurd as manifested in black humor and the existentialist Absurd, with a capital *A*, as it appears in the work of Sartre and Camus, is the philosophical attitude of the protagonist and the author behind him. If both currents reject the notion of inherent "suprapersonal law, dogma, and social order" in the cosmos, existentialism is more affirmative in retaining "a confidence in the dignity and ordering capacity of the individual,"[66] a dignity one rarely if ever finds in the schlemiels and picaros of black humor. If the universe makes no sense in and of itself, according to Camus, at least man exists to make sense of it.

The most extended treatment of the philosophical Absurd appears in Camus's 1940 treatise *The Myth of Sisyphus*. Albert Camus, along with Jean-Paul Sartre, one of the shapers of postwar French existentialist thought, begins this treatise by asking why, in a modern cosmos drained of all purpose, meaning, and direction by the currents of science and history, should an individual not commit suicide? He answers at some length by rejecting all the conventional palliatives, such as religion, duty, and heroism, by which one invests one's life with meaning, offering instead his concept of the Absurd: one should embrace the emptiness of the void, meaninglessness itself, as one's raison d'être, and struggle anyway to survive as a conscious and free individual. As his prime example of the Absurd Man Camus uses the mythological figure of Sisyphus, who for defying the gods was condemned eternally to roll a boulder up a mountain, only to see it perpetually roll down again. Camus sees Sisyphus as happy in this senseless endeavor, which he has taken to heart because it is all he has; the task represents his affirmation as an individual.

Though the limits of the Absurd are left vague by Camus in this treatise, and by his own admission are not fully delineated by it, he does take on those predecessors whose counter-rationalist philosophies seem to possess some links to his, among them Kierkegaard and Kafka. Camus appreciates Kierkegaard's despairing view of the universe, but he scorns his "leap of faith" toward his admittedly incomprehensible God as a retreat from the harsh truth that substitutes for the appropriate "cry of revolt a frantic adherence."[67] In his epilogue to *The Myth of Sisyphus*, "Appendix: Franz Kafka," Camus observes that Kafka's cosmos is Absurd, but that in *The Castle* at least, his hero K. is not, since he continues to seek the acceptance of the Castle, which Camus interprets along with the metaphysical critics as the grace of God.[68] To be truly Absurd, in the full existentialist sense of the word, one must not seek refuge in traditional codes or palliatives of any kind. One must give up hope and live for the struggle alone; only by doing so can one be true to oneself as a free individual in a Godless and meaningless universe.

Despite the comment by Jesse Ritter that began this discussion, little consensus exists as to whether *Catch-22* merely pursues the absurd in the literary Kafka-Céline-West line or reflects the philosophical Absurd of existentialism. Both emphasize the meaninglessness of life, though in Kafka one is allowed to wonder if there is not a divine meaning that one is simply prevented from finding by all those gatekeepers. Both suggest the predominance of the irrational in the universe and the failure of the rational mind to comprehend it.

In interviews Heller has mentioned Kafka and West (along with Nabokov and Céline) as general influences and has freely referred to *Catch-22* as absurd in the literary sense. Allegations of existential Absurdity came early from critics such as Ritter and Vance Ramsey, and from Jean Kennard who flatly asserts, "*Catch-22* reflects a view of the world which is basically that of Jean Paul Sartre and the early Albert Camus. The world has no meaning but is simply there; man is a creature who seeks meaning."[69] Other critics, particularly those who have found traditional religious values in the novel, have denied such assertions, however; for them the absurdity in the novel is technical, a matter of literary form, and not ontological. The issue appears to hinge on two questions: Is ultimate meaning really absent from the world of *Catch-22*? and How does the protagonist accommodate himself to this world?

Looking for now only at the Bologna section of the novel, one must answer the first question with a resounding "Yes." As Yossarian's discussions in the hospital and in bed with Scheisskopf's wife make clear, God is not in his heaven, and even if he were he would only preside incompetently over a cruelly bungled universe, dominated by pointless death and arbitrary injustice. As in Kafka, the human institutions of *Catch-22*—bureaucracies ostensibly created to preserve ideals and order—only end up serving the cosmic facts of death and injustice. How, then, does our hero Yossarian face this fact? Is he merely an absurdist hero in Helen Weinberg's sense, a "passive, rationalistic, or hopelessly ineffectual victim-hero, dominated by his situation rather than creating or acting to change it," like Josef K. of *The Trial*?[70] Is he Camus's Absurd Man, acknowledging the meaninglessness of the cosmos but asserting his individual humanity by struggling in spite of it? Or does he dare to defy the Absurd by continuing to seek purpose in life?

Yossarian is not primarily passive and rationalistic, and he is victimized only unwillingly; in that sense, Clevinger is much more the Kafkan absurdist hero, and indeed his trial in chapter 8 has some things in common with *The Trial* of Josef K. And at this stage in the novel Yossarian can hardly be accused of the Camusian sin of searching for meaning or leaping for the Absolute à la Kierkegaard. He does, however, struggle against those forces that would extinguish his existence and conscious free will, without expecting anything but a temporary triumph; again, the Bologna section dramatizes this point in Yossarian's desperate but ultimately fruitless postponements of the mission, like his determined pummeling of the insensitive Aarfy in the bombardier's compartment. For him, as for Camus's Absurd Man, selfhood—life and free will—is its own reward, and the struggle against the forces that would destroy it, be they natural or man-made, must continue: as in Camus, "though victory is questionable, defeat is not final."[71]

Where Yossarian differs most from the ostensibly Absurd hero Meursault of Camus's existentialist novel *The Stranger*, whose indifference to absolutes leads him to commit a senseless murder that leads to his own execution, is in his lust for life, which prevents him from doing anything so passively stupid. In the picaresque lack of dignity he shares with Céline's Bardamu, in the mad, ironic laughter that accompanies his cry of revolt, the Yossarian of the Bologna chapters is much more like that other Absurd Man that Camus identifies in *The Myth of Sisyphus*—Don Juan.

7

Avignon: The Dialectic of Values

Given the lack of an absolute, divinely inspired value system in the world of *Catch-22,* its venal, Kafkaesque bureaucracies masquerading as guardians of our ideals, and the superficial immorality of its picaresque protagonist, many early reviewers, as noted above, complained that the novel had no moral center. In fact, the third section of the book, bridging its midpoint, brings into focus the sundry value systems, moral and amoral, by which the characters operate.

The division embracing chapters 19 through 25 revolves around the campaign over Avignon in the latter half of summer, beginning with the bombing runs, including Snowden's death and funeral, Yossarian's refusal to wear his uniform and his receiving a medal naked for his bombing of the bridge in the earlier Ferrara mission, and ending chronologically with the week after Cathcart raises the required number of missions to sixty, though, in a typical cycling, this is also where the section begins. In the meantime, the narrative glances back at Ferrara, at the brothel in Rome where Nately's whore resides, and at the history of Milo Minderbinder's rise.

More than the Avignon campaign, however, what sets these chapters apart as a unit is their focus on a few characters who have been in the background of the action up to this point and the values these characters typify; indeed, these seven chapters could be viewed as a discussion among the systems of ethics that strive for dominance in the otherwise valueless universe of the novel.

The characters in question are Colonel Cathcart, Chaplain Tappman, and Milo Minderbinder, with one chapter set aside for the argument on ethics between Nately and Nately's Old Man. The chapters are ordered with a sort of dialectical symmetry: chapter 19 is dominated by Colonel Cathcart facing Chaplain Tappman; chapter 20 belongs to the chaplain; chapter 21 is Cathcart's; chapter 22, Milo's; chapter 23 features Nately and the Old Man; chapter 24 returns to Milo, and chapter 25 is the chaplain's again. The sequence thus runs Cathcart, chaplain, Cathcart; Milo, Old Man, Milo; chaplain. We will take this grouping of chapters and its issues character by character.

THE CHAPLAIN: THE ETHIC OF BELIEF

The chaplain stands at one end of the spectrum of values laid out in these chapters. Chaplain Tappman is probably the most sympathetic character, in the absolute sense, of any in the novel, as Yossarian himself recognizes in the first lines of the book, where he "falls in love" with the chaplain at first sight. As *the* man of God in the story, one would think that, given the sarcastic attacks on God and all conventional attitudes one finds in the book, the chaplain would be an object of particular scorn for the narrative voice. But such is not the case at all. The chaplain is a decent man who scrupulously tries to live by the principles he preaches. He feels compassion for the fighting men he serves; he loves and misses his wife and his three children, and he even feels guilty for taking pills to help him sleep. He feels especially guilty, however, for his ineffectuality, for, though he should represent a moral toehold in the slippery world of the war, the chaplain lets himself be bullied. He is, as he acknowledges to himself, a coward.

We see that this is the case in the first two chapters of this section—in the confrontation between him and Cathcart, in the dialogue between him and Colonel Korn that takes place immediately afterward, and in his exchange with his orderly, Corporal Whitcomb, upon returning to his tent; the chaplain cowers before all of them.

> People with loud voices frightened him. Brave, aggressive men of action like Colonel Cathcart left him feeling helpless and alone. Wherever he went in the army, he was a stranger. Enlisted men and officers did not conduct themselves with him as they conducted themselves with other enlisted men and officers, and even other chaplains were not as friendly toward him as they were toward each other. In a world in which success was the only virtue, he had resigned himself to failure. . . . He was just not equipped to excel. (274)

Like Major Major, that other figure who has done his best to adhere to traditional values, the chaplain is a pariah. Like Yossarian, who as an Assyrian belongs to a no longer existent group, and is thus alienated from the rest of society, the chaplain is an Anabaptist—defined, as Colonel Korn notes, by a negative, "not a Baptist." Like both the other men, the chaplain thus possesses some characteristics of the stereotypical Jewish outcast; indeed, at one point he asks "If they pricked him, didn't he bleed?" (227) in a paraphrase of the Jewish moneylender Shylock in Shakespeare's *Merchant of Venice*.

Colonel Korn, the most overtly cynical and amoral character on Pianosa, has exiled him to a tent in the woods, miles from the units, and made up a complicated rotating mess hall schedule that keeps him out of sight as much as possible. Fortunately, the chaplain does not mind his isolation since he finds his faith easier to justify in his lonely meditations than he does in his attempts to apply it in the real world. His internal wrestling with the problem of faith takes up much of chapter 25, the one entitled "The Chaplain." And his first question, surprising for a religious leader, is "Was there a God?" (274). The chaplain so wants to continue to believe "in the wisdom and justice of an immortal, omnipotent, omniscient, humane, universal, anthropomorphic, English-speaking, Anglo-Saxon, pro-American God," but "[s]o many things were testing his faith" (293). He can see neither wisdom nor justice at work in the world; instead, "prayers went unanswered, and misfortune trampled with equal brutality on the virtuous and the corrupt" (293–294). Indeed, in the world of *Catch-22*, the virtuous—for example, Major Major and the chaplain himself—are more likely than the corrupt to find themselves victims of everything from other people to mere circumstance.

In part his faith is sustained through love, specifically the love he feels for his wife and family, though in his thoughts this translates to fears for their safety from a litany of mortal dangers that rivals Yossarian's, and to "reveries of . . . explicit acts of love-making" with his wife (279). But the chaplain also seeks confirmation of his faith through dubious miracles, or at least moments of mysterious import. It is the chaplain who brings the mention of déjà vu overtly into the narrative, along with the related *jamais vu* and *presque vu*; he is convinced—or wants to be convinced—that the feelings of having experienced something before are tokens of divine mysteries.

He dwells most on one particular occurrence, which has taken place just the month before (July). He was presiding over the funeral of Snowden, at his side the also hapless and victimized Majors Major and Danby, when he saw what he could only take to be a vision: a naked man sitting in a tree overlooking the ceremony. He was trying to account for the apparition when it was joined by another: "a second man clad in a dark mustache and sinister dark garments from head to toe who bent forward ritualistically along the limb of the tree to offer the first man a drink from a brown goblet" (280). As the same sentence notes, it never occurs to the chaplain that there could actually be two men in the tree, one of them naked. We know, from the full narration of the episode in the chapter immediately before, that the naked man is Yossarian, refusing to wear his uniform because Snowden spilled his secret all over it, and that the sinister figure is Milo, offering Yossarian a wad of chocolate-covered cotton.

Since at the time of the funeral the chaplain has not yet met Yossarian, when he does meet him in the hospital he recognizes him in a flash of déjà vu without placing him, and this encounter, too, strikes him as pregnant with mystery. On the day of his visit with Cathcart, the chaplain also finds portentous his encounters and near encounters in the woods: missing Major Major *twice* as they seek each other out to discuss Yossarian's plight, and running into Captain Flume, who is living alone in the woods in fear of Chief White Halfoat. For the chaplain, willing mystical mysteries, this ragged figure becomes "the prophet Flume" when, like some figure of resurrection, he swears he will return to the squadron when winter comes.

Though plainly the evidence that the chaplain accumulates to shore up his shaky faith is false, as the reader knows, it gives the chaplain the shreds he needs to hang on to his belief. In fact, stronger than these elusive miracles is his pure will to believe. Without realizing it, apparently, the chaplain represents the position of those theologians and theocentric philosophers who tread the margins of existentialism, from Kierkegaard through William James to Paul Tillich: Faced with a universe that does not appear to make sense and a God that refuses to reveal Himself, faith must be its own reward. It is impossible to prove God's existence through the use of human reason or by any standards we would consider logical or even moral. Therefore, remembering Kierkegaard, one must apprehend the divine not through reason but through an unreasoning, and thus absurd, leap of commitment. At this point in the narrative, Chaplain Tappman is still half trapped in the desire for empirical evidence of God's existence. But, contrasted with the fact that Yossarian and Dunbar have already given up on God on the basis of the evidence, as noted in the last section, the chaplain's continued search is an indication of belief, even if it is an unfulfilled belief.

In his adherence to traditional Judeo-Christian values, in his willingness to suffer a kind of martyrdom on their behalf, and in his unstinting will to believe, Chaplain Tappman represents one ethical position in the world of *Catch-22*.

COLONEL CATHCART: THE ETHIC OF AMBITION

Colonel Cathcart, as the man responsible for the incessant raising of missions that causes so much woe to Yossarian and his friends, has been viewed by many critics as the evil genius behind much of the plot,

71

even as Antichrist to Yossarian's Christ. While Cathcart is wholly unattractive, however, a close look at his character, as revealed in the Avignon section, shows him to be somewhat less than the dark prime mover of the action.

At the beginning of chapter 19, entitled "Colonel Cathcart," we learn that he is "dashing and dejected, poised and chagrined. He was complacent and insecure, daring in the administrative strategems he employed to bring himself to the attention of his superiors and craven in his concern that his schemes might all backfire" (191–192). He is a tangle of contradictions because, as the narrative relates, he lacks absolutes: "He could measure his progress only in relationship to others, and his idea of excellence was to do something at least as well as all the men his own age who were doing the same thing even better" (192). Further on we read:

> He was tense, irritable, bitter and smug. . . . He collected rumors greedily and treasured gossip. He believed all the news he heard and had faith in none. He was on the alert constantly for every signal, shrewdly sensitive to relationships and situations that did not exist. He was someone in the know who was always striving pathetically to find out what was going on. He was a blustering, intrepid bully who brooded inconsolably over the terrible ineradicable impressions he knew he kept making on people of prominence who were scarcely aware that he was even alive. (193)

Cathcart lives in "an unstable, arithmetical world of black eyes and feathers in his cap, of overwhelming imaginary triumphs and catastrophic imaginary defeats" (193). In short, he is a driven, unhappy man who constantly measures himself against others in a world of his own creation, a world in which his personal sense of worth bears little connection to actuality. In that sense he, like the chaplain, inhabits a self-referential spiritual cosmos. Cathcart's ethic, however, is rooted in far different values. If the chaplain is selfless and thus powerless, Cathcart thinks of nothing but self-aggrandizement; as a colonel in command of the group, he also wields considerable power. His sole desire in life is to become a general, simply because, as Korn says at one point, "Everyone teaches us to aspire to higher things," and, "A general is higher than a colonel" (435).

All of Cathcart's actions come down to this one motive. He tolerates Korn's cynical assistance only because Korn is more clever than he is at coming up with schemes, and Cathcart hates him for it. He raises his men's missions solely to get the attention of his commanding officers; he calls the chaplain into his office to have him lead prayers before missions in order to get into the *Saturday Evening Post.* He maintains a drafty house in the hills at Korn's recommendation in order to feed rumors of orgies in the hopes that one of the generals he wants to impress will take note and ask to join in. Only the chance of promotion could induce him to consider sexual activity: "the colonel was certainly not going to waste his time and energy making love to beautiful women unless there was something in it for him" (216).

In his study of black humor, Max Schulz suggests that Colonel Cathcart suffers the angst of the *Massenmensch*[72]—the painful anxiety of mass man—so acutely described in *The Organization Man* and *The Lonely Crowd.* In the terms of David Riesman, author of the latter book, Cathcart is an "other-directed" person, soulless and conformist. He has yielded the power over his life to social forces he can only barely control and is forever terrified of displeasing his chosen authority figures. In fact, despite the bureaucratic power he himself wields, Cathcart is a Kafkan figure, victimized by a system and an ethic he accepts as valid, victimized indeed by that very acceptance. He allows himself to be subjected to the whims of mysterious gods, gods with names like Dreedle and Peckem, and he quails even before subordinate powers he does not understand, like the Olympian Major ——— de Coverley and the demonic, oft-mentioned Yossarian.

Cathcart's problem with the arbitrary authority of his gods comes forth in this section, appropriately, with the juxtaposition of General Dreedle and that man of God, Chaplain Tappman. Cathcart remembers as one of his black eyes a series of episodes in which Dreedle found the chaplain in the officers' club. On the first occasion Dreedle remarks, "That's really a fine thing when a man of God begins hanging around a place like this with a bunch of dirty drunks and gamblers" (291). Taking the remark as disapproving, Cathcart moves to have the chaplain thrown out, only to discover that Dreedle is sincere about it being "a fine thing." The next time they appear in the club together, however, Dreedle makes the same statement in disapproval, throwing Cathcart off balance again. Cathcart ultimately blames the chaplain, finding fault in him because "it was impossible to predict *how* General Dreedle would react each time he saw him" (291).

Similar misunderstanding characterizes almost all of Cathcart's dealings with Dreedle. A humorous example is the piece of Abbott and Costello dialogue between them in the officers' club in which Cathcart, unable to follow Dreedle's train of thought, confuses the chaplain with Colonel Korn (292–93).

Dreedle is an old war horse, a career Army man who is accustomed to exercising authority and does not even realize it has limits, as when he arbitrarily sentences men to be shot, reminiscent of Alice's Red Queen's "Off with their heads!" His sole nemesis is General Peckem, commander of Special Services, who wants the greater power of Dreedle's job. Peckem is a man more to Cathcart's liking, a man of ambition who will do anything to advance his own cause and who is thus more understandable to Cathcart. Cathcart strives to impress Peckem not because he has to but because he wants to; Peckem is the sort of suave, self-promoting, upwardly mobile individual that Cathcart envisions himself to be. Cathcart strives to impress Dreedle because he must, Dreedle being his commanding officer. Dreedle thinks in terms of military targets and winning the war; Peckem in terms of aerial photographs and "tight bomb patterns." The lines between them are drawn on matters of substance and style, with Peckem coming down on the side of style. He wants men to wear dress uniforms into combat; Dreedle does not care whether the men wear uniforms at all, (as he demonstrates when he hands a medal to the naked Yossarian), as long as they fight.

In the struggle between Dreedle and Peckem, between the old Army man and the new organization man, Cathcart allies himself implicitly with the latter. If for Dreedle war is an end in itself, for Cathcart and Peckem it is merely an excuse for self-perpetuation and aspiration.

MILO: THE ETHIC OF CAPITALISM

Milo Minderbinder is one of the most memorable characters in the novel, a consummate entrepreneur who builds an international business empire over the course of the book's action. When he first appears in operation in chapter 7, dealing in figs and torn bedsheets, he seems a comical, harmless hustler, somewhat in the vein of one of his undoubted models, the con Applejack Katz in Algren's *The Man with the Golden Arm*. Though imprisoned, Katz "had half a dozen minor projects going, involving the bartering of nutmeg for Bull Durham, of Bull Durham for nutmeg, and of emory for the manufacture of something he called a 'glin wheel,' a sort of homemade cigarette lighter. It was also his daily concern, while working beside Frankie on the mangle roller, to steal the paraffin wax off the rollers for the making of candles, which he sold clandestinely to the harder cons upstairs."[73] Indeed, Milo stands at the end of a long American tradition of such literary con men.[74]

Except for a few scenes concerning the beginnings of his career, Milo has remained more or less in the background of the novel up to the middle of chapter 22, "Milo the Mayor." There he leads Yossarian and Orr on a whirlwind tour of the Mediterranean, wheeling and dealing while keeping them out of the way with prearranged whores. Although Yossarian finds himself misused and neglected by Milo, he cannot help being amused and impressed by Milo's entrepreneurial savvy and the increasing influence it has gained him. At the end of the ordeal, Yossarian still considers Milo his friend.

It is in this chapter that we learn how ornate Milo's multifarious business dealings are, that the profits go into Milo's syndicate, and that "everyone has a share." We also learn here that Milo, because of his success as a capitalist, has been made the mayor of various Sicilian towns, "the Vice-Shah of Oran, . . . the Caliph of Baghdad, the Imam of Damascus, and the Sheik of Araby. Milo was the corn god, the rain god and the rice god in backward regions . . . and deep inside the jungles of Africa, he intimated with becoming modesty, large graven images of his mustached face could be found overlooking primitive stone altars red with human blood" (244).

Milo is thus not only the prime mercantile power of the Mediterranean theater, but a political and even spiritual power as well. If anyone represents an Antichrist figure, it is he, as he shows during his temptation scene at Snowden's funeral. And yet, ironically, Milo is highly moral in his own way; unlike, say, Cathcart and Korn, he does possess a concrete and absolute set of values. For instance, he expresses a conventional puritanical distaste for Yossarian and Orr's whoring on their mercantile excursion, even though he contracts for the whores himself. He refuses on principle, as a good capitalist, to deal with communists, though he has no such reservations toward dealing with Nazis. Heller sees Milo as being more "horrifyingly dangerous" for having this "mental and moral simplicity" and lacking "evil intent."[75] As Leon F. Seltzer notes, Milo fully represents the "moral insanity" of this world, the inability to recognize the difference between moral behavior and immoral behavior that is permitted, indeed, even encouraged, by the capitalist apotheosis of private profit.[76]

The profit motive stands at the pinnacle of Milo's concrete value system, dominating all else. It takes precedence over everything from loyalty to his friends, as we see in the insensitive treatment Yossarian and Orr receive at Milo's hands in chapter 22, to disloyalty to his country, as we learn in chapter 24 ("Milo"). It is there that the episodes of Milo contracting with the Germans to attack American forces, foreshadowed earlier, are described in detail, though both have taken place the summer before the Avignon campaign.

The first is the Orvieto deal, in which Milo contracts with the U.S. Air Force to bomb a gun emplacement and with a German antiaircraft division to shoot the planes down. He realizes a "fantastic profit" from both sides, and genuinely fails to understand Yossarian's argument against dealing with death and the enemy. Milo's sincere counterargument is that he needs the profit to make up the losses from his ill-advised cornering of the entire Egyptian cotton crop. And Milo would never renege on his agreement to do so, because in his honorbound devotion to capitalist values, "a contract was a contract" (264). Immediately after this darkly humorous event the narrative segues into the even worse episode in which Milo bombs his own base. The scene is graphically delineated, with men running in terror and wounded men screaming everywhere. Amid this mayhem, we are told, in a tossed-off aside at odds with the general horror of the event, that the crews "spared the landing strip and the mess halls so that they could land safely when their work was done and enjoy a hot snack before retiring" (264).

For a moment it looks as though Milo's willingness to go so far to protect his investments and his ethic of enterprise promises his doom. Cathcart is livid, seeing this incident, of course, as a major "black eye." Word soon filters back to the American public, and everyone from congressmen to women's groups call for Milo's punishment—that is, until he opens his books and reveals what a tremendous profit he has made from the deal. No one, especially in the United States of America, can argue with a successful application of the capitalist ethic. Vindicated, Milo suggests that governments should get out of the conduct of war altogether and "leave the whole field to private industry" (266).

The preeminence of Milo's ethic of profit is neatly symbolized in the passage where we are told that the planes he receives from the military for his syndicate are emblazoned with emblems "illustrating such laudable ideals as Courage, Might, Justice, Truth, Liberty, Love, Honor and Patriotism," which Milo has his mechanics paint out in flat white and replace with his own logo (259). He does likewise with the swastikas on the German planes he has added to his fleet. Milo's ethic crosses all international boundaries, overwhelms all belief systems—except communism, with which he refuses to deal—and dominates them.

That there is no trace of cynicism in Milo's approach to his enterprise is underlined in the "Milo" chapter in his exchange with Yossarian, who is sitting naked in the tree overlooking the funeral. The tree, which Yossarian says is the "tree of life . . . and of knowledge of good and evil, too" (269), is only a chestnut tree to Milo, who sells chestnuts and thus would know. Milo proves himself further impervious to any traditional concepts of good and evil. The tragedy implicit in Snowden's funeral means little before the glut of cotton on Milo's hands. When Yossarian suggests that Milo sell his cotton to the government, Milo at first objects on principle: "The government has no business in business." But within that paragraph he argues himself quite readily into the position that "the government does have the responsibility of buying all the Egyptian cotton I've got that no one else wants so that I can make a profit" (272). When Yossarian suggests he bribe the government to make sure it takes the cotton, Milo at first reacts with righteous indignation, but immediately convinces himself that since there is no law against making a profit, that motive takes precedent over lesser crimes. Yossarian cynically offers Milo other arguments he can use to convince the government, arguments which Milo promptly makes his own with a sense of absolute certainty that Yossarian does not share. As Yossarian observes, "You almost make it sound true. . . . You do it with just the right amount of conviction." But for Milo, "It is true" (273). And when Milo repeats the slogan of his cartel, "What is good for M & M Enterprises is good for the country," he believes so every bit as much as Charles E. Wilson believed in the statement regarding GM that Milo is paraphrasing.

In his own way, Milo is as much a true believer as the chaplain, even more so, in fact, since Milo is not plagued by the metaphysical doubts that besiege the chaplain's faith. Of course, in the world of *Catch-22*, as in the real world, the ethic of profit operates with far greater success than the ethic of religious faith; so Milo wins a justification of his worldview that the chaplain can only dream of.

The only scene of the novel in which the chaplain and Milo appear together is Snowden's funeral, described twice near the end of this section. It could be considered the climactic scene of this section, in fact, since it not only brings together the chaplain's will to believe and Milo's ethic of profit but also arranges both around Yossarian. Yossarian is, of course, sitting naked in the tree overlooking the cemetery; Snowden's death has been for him the climactic moment of the Avignon campaign, around which this section is built.

In his essay, cited earlier, Victor J. Milne maintains that Yossarian represents in this scene "a second Adam in naked innocence, [who] rejects temptation in a ludicrous re-enactment of the story of the Fall of Man."[77] Yossarian's identification of the tree with the tree of Eden as well as the chaplain's visionary version of the scene justify Milne's interpretation, though Heller does deflate the spiritual significance of the moment by putting Yossarian's version of the event after the chaplain's. Still, Yossarian's rejection of the temptation Milo offers—the temptation "to submit to absurd exploitation" and thus sanction it for all the men—suggests his wider rejection of Milo's, and the world's, ruling ethic.[78] But whether Yossarian represents a Christ-like figure, as Milne also suggests, is less certain.

Ironically, though Heller thought that, after Yossarian, the chaplain was the second most memorable character in the novel, he learned to his surprise that for most readers it was Milo.[79] Even here Milo proved more powerful than the humble man of God.

NATELY'S OLD MAN: THE ETHIC OF SURVIVAL

Chapter 23—"Nately's Old Man"—consists almost entirely of Nately's argument with the cynical old Roman, framed by descriptions of the route to the brothel where the Old Man lives and of Nately's family. The exchange between Nately and the Old Man is another of the oft-cited set pieces of the novel. It is customarily regarded as a confrontation between the idealism of Nately and the pragmatic survivalism of the Old Man, with the latter emerging clearly victorious. This conversation, however, is only one sally in the dialectic on ethics that continues in one form or another throughout the rest of the novel.

Nately, like Clevinger, is a dope—a young man with many advantages of upbringing and with a deep and romantic commitment to traditional ideals like those that Milo whites off of his planes. In Nately's case, romanticism has led him to fall hopelessly in love with an Italian prostitute who responds to his attentions with sleepy indifference, suggesting, once again, that his perception of reality has little to do with empirical fact. This variation on the will to believe informs the main thrust of Nately's side of the argument with the Old Man.

The Old Man is described as a slovenly Bacchus, an old pagan god of hedonism seated amid the naked voluptuousness of a dozen prostitutes. He reminds Nately of his own old man—his wealthy, gentlemanly, conventionally bigoted and snobbish father—because, in the inverted logic of the novel, "the two were nothing at all alike" (250). Using that same inverted logic, the Old Man opens his side of the argument with his insistence that Italy, having already lost the war, is doing very well now, whereas Germany and America, still struggling for victory, are both doing poorly; Italian soldiers are no longer dying, but German and American soldiers are. For the Old Man, success is synonymous with survival.

The Old Man has, by his own admission, no principles. When the Germans occupied Italy, he celebrated; when the Americans rolled in, he celebrated. Nately is shocked by this cynical lack of loyalty and patriotism, by the Old Man's contempt for the whole idea of countries and ideals to fight for. But at the end of every line of reasoning stands the Old Man's ultimate argument: "I am a hundred and seven years old." In the process, he inverts or deflates all of the clichéd sentiments of the younger man. "Anything worth living for," says Nately, "is worth dying for." To which the Old Man answers, "Anything worth dying for . . . is worth living for" (253). To Nately's, "it's better to die on one's feet than live on one's knees," he replies, "It is better to *live* on one's feet than die on one's knees" (254). And he suggests that Nately ask his friends, Yossarian and Dunbar, implying that they will agree.

The Old Man embodies the picaresque, Célinesque principle that one must lie or die. At first glance Yossarian and Dunbar do indeed seem to share his amoral survivalism, as they share his lusty, life-affirming hedonism; Yossarian has proved willing, as is dramatically shown in the Bologna section, to do anything to hold on to life, and Dunbar cultivates boredom to make his life longer since, "What else is there?" (40). In fact, James Nagel has suggested that the Old Man represents a sort of spiritual guide for Yossarian, proposing an ethic that he gradually endorses over the course of the novel.[20] As the later sections of the novel and the pertinent discussion will show, however, the Old Man does not get the last word on Yossarian's ethics.

If Colonel Cathcart or, better yet, Colonel Korn represents the cynicism of those in power, the Old Man represents the cynicism of the powerless. Both ethical systems are relativistic; that is, in each case individual behavior is determined by the environment—for Cathcart and Korn, environment dictates whatever is necessary for self-advancement; for the Old Man, it dictates whatever is conducive to increased years. But the Old Man's ethic is life-promoting whereas Cathcart's is life-destroying. A similar pairing holds true for the two value systems represented in this section that are absolute as opposed to relativistic: the chaplain's, tied to belief and life-promoting, and Milo's, tied to "the squalid, corrupting indignities of the profit motive" (321) and life-destroying.

At this point in the chronology, Yossarian naturally stands opposed to the ethic of Cathcart and Korn, who are out to get him killed, though he still regards Milo, with bemused respect, as a friend. He has not yet met the chaplain, who as a believer in traditional religious values would seem to be furthest from Yossarian and Dunbar; by allowing himself to be victimized by those more powerful than he while remaining faithful to a conventional code, the chaplain should be in the "dope" category with Clevinger and Nately. But Yossarian "falls in love" with him at first sight, and he and Dunbar treat him with respect, perhaps recognizing that his values do interface with theirs, in that they promote life.

If the ethical stances set forth in the Avignon section appear clearly delineated, Yossarian's relationship to them is less so. From here on, our antihero becomes the focus of a morality play with these sundry opposed value systems—power, profit, belief, and survival—vying for his sensibility and sense of self. From here on, too, the novel becomes more or less chronological. It is as though Avignon represents a knotting together of all the tangled threads of the earlier sections; thus, the Avignon mission, coming at the midpoint of the novel and climaxing in Snowden's funeral, does stand as a possible moral center around which other events revolve, a divine fulcrum, the full significance of which only becomes clear later in the novel.

8

Rome: Toward the Eternal City

So far in the novel, the narrative has operated in circles, going around the same events twice or even more, and each time adding another level of information or significance. Thus, the mad, illogical humor of the first chapters, after setting the fundamental rhetorical rules for this cosmos, is overlain in the Bologna section by a pall of death, injustice, and meaninglessness, leaving a blank moral slate upon which the ethical dialectic of the Avignon section can be laid out but not resolved. Each time around the reader has learned more about events mentioned earlier and more about the characters, and the story has continued to darken in tone, so that what was laughable earlier, like the soldier in white or Milo's business dealings, is later less laughable and more thematically significant.

The section of the novel embracing chapters 26 through 37 represents a real shift in the direction of the narrative; the repetitive cycles end for the most part and are replaced by largely chronological plot action, beginning around the time Cathcart raises the required missions to sixty, and thus roughly at the time of the chaplain's meeting with him in the Avignon section, not long after his first meeting Yossarian in chapter 1. From here the story continues more or less in a straight line from late summer through fall, largely focusing once again on Yossarian's immediate circle on Pianosa, but with important side excursions to Rome and to General Peckem's war on General Dreedle. With the cessation of the earlier characteristic cycles, this section also ceases the concomitant superimpositions; instead of bringing further issues and themes to the material, it extrapolates from those already introduced in the earlier groupings. Déjà vu continues to function in this section, but mostly through the introduction of figures and episodes that closely mimic earlier ones. Everything, however, whether old or new, continues to darken in tone and grow in significance.

A prime example is the central episode of the first chapter of this grouping, entitled "Aarfy." Here is where Aarfy, the incompetent navigator, leads Yossarian's plane into flak over Leghorn following the weekly milk run to Parma. As Yossarian opens his eyes to the horror of possible sudden death, Aarfy looks on in bemusement in a scene reminiscent of the air fight during Bologna. This time, however, Yossarian finds himself even more threatened by death, being immobilized by a wound in the groin. Fearing that he has been castrated by the flak (Heller's original intention, according to early notes of the novel[81]), he screams to Aarfy; this time Aarfy is not only deaf to Yossarian, he is apparently unable to see, with his "blind" grin, the blood pooling under Yossarian's leg. Once more Aarfy stands in for the brute indifference of the absurd cosmos of *Catch-22,* which if anything is worsening as the narrative proceeds (indeed, the Latin root of *absurd* means *deaf*). As Yossarian observes to himself while passing out: "He was dying, and no one took notice" (297).

The wound does give Yossarian his first legitimate reason for entering the hospital, however. And in this déjà vu sanctuary a few familiar motifs return.

THE HOSPITAL AGAIN: IDENTITY AND INSANITY

The first chapter of the section ends with Yossarian and a malingering Dunbar merrily changing identities in the ward by changing beds. This is another instance, like Caleb Major really being some stranger named Major Major, like Yossarian being a dying soldier named Giuseppe, of names taking on lives of their own and controlling individuals, that is, of signifiers dominating the signified. Indeed, with punning relevance Dunbar is actually one A. Fortiori when Yossarian first sees him.

Howard J. Stark quotes *Black's Law Dictionary* to point out that ". . . *a fortiori* is a term used in logic 'to denote an argument to the effect that because one ascertained fact exists, therefore another, which is included in it, or analogous to it, and which is less improbable, unusual, or surprising, must also exist.'"[82] In the immediate case, since Yossarian finds Dunbar in A. Fortiori's bed, he is A. Fortiori, and when Yossarian replaces Homer Lumley, he becomes Homer Lumley, "who felt like vomiting and was covered suddenly with a clammy sweat" (300). The same practice of rooting all conclusions in preordained facts has been characteristic of events in the entire novel: Mudd could not have been killed in combat because he had not been officially admitted to the squadron; Clevinger must be guilty or he would not have been charged; concern for personal safety is the operation of a rational mind, therefore anyone who asks to be grounded is by definition sane.

Yossarian's sanity and identity both come into question after he and Dunbar mash Nurse Duckett and invent a shared dream in which Yossarian holds a live fish in his hand. Yossarian soon finds himself confronting the psychiatrist Major Sanderson. Not surprisingly, given the world of *Catch-22*, Sanderson comes across as crazier than his patient. He presumes deep psychological reasons for Yossarian refusing a cigarette and disliking fish, despite obvious explanations. He blatantly shows insecurities and fears of his own. He seems to think that Dunbar is an invention of Yossarian's onto which he projects his darker side (which may be close to the truth). He sneers at Yossarian and verbally attacks him in a wholly unprofessional manner, and begs him to dream a genuinely sadistic sex dream. And, a fortiori, he gives precedence to names over facts when he insists that Yossarian is not Yossarian with a wounded thigh but A. Fortiori with a stone in his salivary gland; he ignores the stitches in Yossarian's leg in favor of "an official Army record" (307).

Ultimately, Sanderson restates the insane inversions that underlie the whole world of the novel, accusing Yossarian of being mentally ill because he cannot adjust to warfare and sudden, violent death. Furthermore, Sanderson vituperates, "You're antagonistic to the idea of being robbed, exploited, degraded, humiliated or deceived." He declares Yossarian crazy because he is depressed by misery, ignorance, persecution, violence, greed, crime, and other ills. And when Yossarian calls him crazy in return, he sputters that calling someone crazy "is a typically sadistic and vindictive paranoiac reaction," just before he calls Yossarian crazy again (312). In fact, believing Yossarian too crazy for combat, Sanderson orders A. Fortiori sent home.

Finishing off this replay of the madness theme is Yossarian's renewed assault on Doc Daneeka, in a déjà vu reminder of their Catch-22 conversation; to Yossarian's insistence that he has been declared insane and thus unfit for combat, Daneeka simply replies with the question: "Who else will go?" (314).

In fact, the very next line—opening the next chapter—is, "McWatt went, and McWatt was not crazy" (314). If the return of the madness motif seems simply redundant at this point, this set of chapters gives insanity a far more serious edge than it had in the novel's opening section. The comment about McWatt, for instance, comes at the beginning of a dialogue between Yossarian and Dobbs, who in an earlier scene had insanely begged Yossarian to give him permission to kill Cathcart. Their positions are reversed now, with Yossarian, having learned that Cathcart plans to volunteer the men for Bologna again, begging Dobbs to kill Cathcart while Dobbs tries to calm him down. In fact, Yossarian begins to threaten many people with murder in these chapters, including friends like Orr and McWatt. The scene with McWatt is particularly chilling: during a routine training flight with Yossarian on board, McWatt begins stunt flying low over the ground, as is his wont. A frightened and angry Yossarian, after failing to find a .45, simply slips his bare hands around McWatt's throat. Afterward, when McWatt seriously tells an ashamed Yossarian, "you sure must be in pretty bad shape," the reader trusts his judgment on the state of Yossarian's wits far more than that of Sanderson (342).

The last such episode occurs during the drunken Thanksgiving celebration of chapter 34, when Yossarian awakes to the sound of machine gun fire and cringes in mortal terror under his cot until he realizes that this ostensible threat to his life resulted from celebrating soldiers. "He wanted to kill, he wanted to murder," we are told. "He was angrier than he had ever been before, angrier even than when he had slid his hands around McWatt's neck to strangle him" (370). This time he does have a .45 at hand, and with it he heads for the machine gun emplacement. When Nately attempts to restrain him, Yossarian "drove his fist squarely into Nately's delicate young face as hard as he could," and only fails to hit him a second time because Nately collapses out of sight (370).

Significantly, even though Yossarian misses the gunners, he does run into Dunbar at the emplacement, also with .45 in hand and murder on his mind. Like Yossarian, Dunbar has been driven to the brink of genuine insanity by the struggle to preserve self in the face of the war and the morally insane bureaucracy conducting it. Dunbar has already gone further than Yossarian in some respects; in a courageous if mad act, given the rules of this world, he refuses to participate in a morally repulsive mission by dropping his bombs far from the site. His personality seems to have suffered permanent damage; he is if anything more edgy and dour than his friend. He "seldom laughed any more and seemed to be wasting away. He snarled belligerently at superior officers, even at Major Danby, and was crude and surly and profane even in front of the chaplain. . ." (339).

It should not be too surprising that Dunbar's mounting madness parallels Yossarian's own. Throughout the novel Yossarian and Dunbar have been paired, though of course Dunbar's role is nowhere near as great as Yossarian's. From the first chapter of the novel the two men have shared a consistent viewpoint on life—and death. Both are determined "to live forever or die in the attempt." For both, life is all there is to live for, a feeling which Dunbar carries to the extreme of seeking out boring and unpleasant situations to make his life go by more slowly. Both argue with Clevinger in the early chapters of the book, and they are linked as survivalist allies by the Old Man in his arguments with Nately. Together they seek to avoid duty or otherwise discomfort authority by malingering in the hospital or perpetuating episodes such as the moaning in the Avignon briefing. And though he appears to share Yossarian's affection for the chaplain, Dunbar is even more resolute than Yossarian on the insistence that "There is no God."

Dunbar could be taken as an aspect of Yossarian's Gestalt, a shadow or doppelgänger who represents the existential bottom line of his personality: committed to life at all costs, antiauthority and pro-freedom, angered and horrified by the void and the many in power who seem determined to drive them there. Dunbar's increasing sour-ness and withdrawal, therefore, underlines Yossarian's more serious approach in this section to the aspects of this world that are bothering him.

The climax to Dunbar's madness comes in chapter 34, appropri-ately back in the hospital, while he and Yossarian are malingering to keep the injured Nately company. Suddenly the soldier in white reap-pears, driving Dunbar to the screaming certainty that the dead man in plaster of the earlier chapters has come back. Though he is not exactly the same size, he does have the familiar solid whiteness about him, and the black hole over the mouth leading into a "lightless, unstirring void," (375) and the jars of clear fluid dripping into and out of him. Dunbar is certain this time that there is no one inside. He sends the entire ward into an infectious panic with his insane terror, until he is finally dragged away by MPs and armed doctors.

Yossarian shares his terror, though he seems more horrified by Dunbar's shrill, uncontrolled reaction to the soldier than by the figure itself. If Yossarian does not reach the same level of frenzy, it is only because Dunbar so well embodies that part of him that fears the emp-tiness; Dunbar rages for both of them, goes mad for both of them, and is disappeared for both of them.

The soldier in white must symbolize for Yossarian what he does for Dunbar: the ultimate reification of the human being. The soldier in white is man stripped of spirit, stripped of flesh ("There's no one inside!"), reduced to inorganic components of plaster, steel, and glass, with watery fluid being cycled pointlessly through them. The soldier in white is like death in that sense; worse, he represents a sort of death-in-life, the human stripped of individualism, identity, mobility, free will, and purpose.

If the war threatens to kill off Yossarian and his friends, the military institutions of *Catch-22* threaten this sort of death-in-life for them, the stealing away of their individual identities. As a small, nearby instance, there is Nurse Cramer's remark during the hospital stay of chapter 26 that Yossarian belongs to the U.S. government, and that his injured leg is as much government property as "a gear or a bedpan" (300). This is the same chapter in which Yossarian and Dunbar themselves experiment with abusing power and blurring personal identity by trading beds with non-coms.

One of the strongest reminders in this section of how thoroughly these institutions and their a fortiori structures can obliterate human identity comes with Doc Daneeka's reported death in chapter 30. Having been signed on to McWatt's plane at the time that McWatt accidentally clips Kid Sampson in half and then flies into the mountain, Daneeka is officially, on paper, dead, even though he is clearly standing on the ground when the crash takes place. The narrative observes that Sergeant Towser, who has already been much troubled by Mudd—the dead man in Yossarian's tent whose things cannot be removed because he did not officially report for duty before he was killed and is therefore not officially dead—will have an even greater problem with Doc Daneeka, who though officially dead "most certainly was there and gave every indication of proving a still thornier administrative problem" (350).

Daneeka resolutely struggles for life for some time thereafter, but he has only the fact of his physical existence to stand up against a mountain of official paperwork. Informed of his death by Sergeant Towser, his orderlies Gus and Wes turn him out of the medical tent. Cathcart and Korn refuse to let him show himself around the base. And his wife back home quickly overcomes her doubt and grief in the face of multiplying letters, life insurance policies, and burial payoffs from various organizations, despite two impassioned letters recognizably in her husband's hand. The last blow at Daneeka, and one typically negligent, even in "death," of his individual identity, is the official letter of condolence the wife receives from Cathcart, consisting of Whitcomb's impersonal formula: *Words cannot express the deep personal grief I experienced when your husband, son, father or brother was killed, wounded, or reported missing in action.*

Other moments that illustrate the objectification of human identity appear in the neighboring chapters. For instance, when Yossarian, Dunbar, and friends raid an apartment where Nately's whore is being held by a group of naked generals, Yossarian and friends are only able to assert power over them because the latter are out of uniform. Without the outward and visible signs of their authority, they lack authority as superior officers; they themselves casually acknowledge as much, even praising the junior officers for their strategic cleverness in throwing the uniforms out the windows. Without the uniforms, the generals are merely fat men with pillows.

It is significant too that after the episode of the soldier in white Dunbar is not just court-martialed, or even executed, but "disappeared," with that word's overtones of complete obliteration. The term reminds one of Orwell's *1984*, another of Heller's subliminal influences. As in *1984*, the control of reality and thus the control of people is rooted in large part in the control of language, and the society of Big Brother is perfectly capable of erasing, through the manipulation of information and thought, any trace of a person's existence. When Nurse Duckett tells Yossarian that "they were going to disappear Dunbar," Yossarian observes, "It doesn't make sense. It isn't even good grammar" (376). But as the novel has demonstrated, those in the positions of power in this world set the rules of discourse and through them the syllogisms of allowable thought and behavior; thus, they also set the standards for human identity and nonidentity. The reification of the human being is therefore connected to the reification of language: the sundering of words from their meanings, of names from individuals, of signifier from signified.

This issue also surfaces in the main subplot of this section, namely, the war for control of the war being conducted by General Peckem—a war of words.

PECKEM'S WAR, PECKEM'S PEOPLE

General Peckem, it will be recalled, has been battling all along against his own enemy, General Dreedle, for control of the Mediterranean theater of operations. He is the erudite-sounding, superficially witty, style-conscious head of Special Services, in charge of entertainment and recreation for the troops. A devotee of the ethic of ambition, he besieges the Mediterranean command with requests to have combat operations transferred to Special Services on the grounds that bombing is the most special service of all.

It is he who, in earlier chapters, gives orders that men should wear dress uniforms into combat in order to make a better impression if killed or captured, that tents on the Mediterranean bases should be oriented patriotically toward the Washington Monument, and that bombs should be dropped in "tight bomb patterns" to make good aerial photographs. Dreedle, "who ran a fighting outfit," cares nothing at all for such matters of mere style and is infuriated, though helpless, when he finds Peckem's memoranda crossing his own. If Peckem fails on occasion, it is only because Wintergreen, the oft-busted enlisted man who runs the Mediterranean mail room, dislikes the writing style of Peckem's memoranda and usually tosses them out on those grounds. Peckem moves his headquarters to Rome soon after the Allies conquer it, while Dreedle remains on Corsica. Peckem's move to the Eternal City helps place him near the institutional center of power of classical Empire and medieval church, and helps tie together the other Roman threads that wind through this section.

Peckem's interest in tight bomb patterns—which by his own admission is a whim on his part that, to his amusement, has been picked up by ambitious underlings like Cathcart—leads to a mission that represents a turning point for Yossarian's circle. When the group is ordered to bomb a defenseless Italian village, supposedly to make a road block but really to make good aerial photographs, the men, especially Dunbar, balk. An uncomfortable Major Danby tries to back up Headquarters on faith during the pre-mission briefing, but even McWatt, who usually enjoys flying missions, does not like the sound of this one. Colonel Korn, with typical cynicism, threatens the men with another mission to Bologna or Ferrara; he knows their desire for self-preservation will shut them up. Korn, after having made a vigorous case for the road block, ends with a characteristic inversion: "We don't care about the roadblock. . . . Colonel Cathcart wants to come out of this mission with a good clean aerial photograph he won't be ashamed to send through channels" (337). But it is during this mission that Dunbar completely washes his hands of the war by purposely dropping his bombs miles from the target, while Yossarian has numbed himself so that "he no longer gave a damn where his bombs fell" (339).

The reappearance of Scheisskopf as a colonel attached to Peckem brings in another figure who prefers form over content, style over substance, and who is more than willing to use human beings as objects. Scheisskopf, one recalls from chapter 8, is a genuine fool who cares about nothing but parades; we only have the narrator's word for it that he accepts the ethic of ambition (71).

The parades themselves are absolutely worthless in every way, as worthless as the pennants the squadrons win for doing best in the parades: "all they signified was that the owner had done something of no benefit to anyone more capably than everyone else" (73). Yet nothing is more important to Scheisskopf, who spends long hours every night manipulating chocolate soldiers and plastic cowboys while his wife lusts for his company in bed and, always disappointed, seduces his cadets. In planning for the perfect formation, Scheisskopf considers "nailing the twelve men in each rank to a long two-by-four beam of seasoned oak to keep them in line" (74), but gives up the idea only because "making a ninety-degree turn would have been impossible without nickel-alloy swivels inserted in the small of every man's back," and Scheisskopf doubts he can get the cooperation of the quartermaster and the surgeons (75). When he discovers the arcane regulation about marching men keeping their hands close to the thigh, his "first thought had been to . . . sink pegs of nickel alloy into each man's thighbones and link them to the wrists by strands of copper wire," but he neither has the time nor access to so much good copper wire (75).

In short, for Scheisskopf the men have no more reality as flesh-and-blood human beings than the toy figures he manipulates in private. They are simply objects to be moved around on the playing board of the parade field, to be drilled and nailed and screwed, if possible. Material, not ethical, considerations are all that stand between him and his wishes.

Nothing stands in the way of his promotion to higher rank, however, and he comes to Peckem a full colonel. He is still obsessed with parades, and is so immune to the usual protocol of self-aggrandizement that he fails to appreciate any of Peckem's customary witticisms. Even Peckem's love of meaningless style does not extend to Scheisskopf's obsession, and Scheisskopf must content himself with scheduling and canceling nonexistent parades, again distancing the relationship of word and thing.

Another link in this paper chain of command is Wintergreen. Technically, Wintergreen is at the very bottom of the military hierarchy. Due to his penchant for going AWOL and other acts of blatant disobedience, he is forever being demoted. For most of the novel, he is ex-P.F.C. Wintergreen, though we also see him promoted to ex-corporal and even ex-sergeant. As an official underling he receives the most humble jobs, from the ditch-digging he receives as punishment at Lowery Field to the mail-sorting he performs in the Mediterranean.

True to the ironic inversions of *Catch-22*, however, Wintergreen turns out to be among the most powerful figures of the novel. In a world in which the word, as interpreted by the official bureaucracy, takes precedence over the thing, Wintergreen manipulates the words. As already noted, he gives Dreedle the advantage in the war of memos between the generals by throwing out most of Peckem's prolix communications. He has the final say on which communications make it across the Atlantic, and thus has much to do with Daneeka's "death." He even threatens to cancel Eisenhower's D-Day invasion of Europe until Eisenhower commits more armored divisions.

In the same way that Wintergreen can single-handedly veto the war effort and Peckem's ambitions, and can shuffle human lives around as so many pieces of mail, he also proves capable of beating Milo at his own game. No sooner has Milo set up his cartel than Wintergreen goes into competition with him, underselling him on a number of items and cornering the market in Zippo lighters while Milo languishes with Egyptian cotton. Unlike Milo, Wintergreen holds not even the profit motive as a sacred ideal; he is a thorough cynic with no interests beyond himself. More than once he refuses to help Yossarian, and his arguments are completely shoddy and self-serving, as in the previously mentioned discussion regarding Yossarian's patriotic wartime duty to risk his life in combat and Wintergreen's to make a profit selling Zippo lighters. As a complete cynic Wintergreen has little trouble taking the institutional side against Yossarian, since he knows where the power is.

As the linchpin of the paper bureaucracy Wintergreen ultimately ends up being a member of the Roman triumvirate that heads the war at the finish of this section. In chapter 37 we see General Peckem successful in his bid to replace General Dreedle as commander of combat operations. His victory quickly becomes pyrrhic, however, when his other campaign—to have combat operations placed under Special Services—also succeeds. Unfortunately, in leaving Special Services for the combat command, Peckem has left Scheisskopf, now promoted to general, in charge, and thus in charge of the conduct of the war. Of course, all that Scheisskopf is interested in is having everybody march. During this chapter, entitled "General Scheisskopf," at two pages the briefest in the book, we see the entire official military bureaucracy inverted in one blow. The acknowledged imbecile Scheisskopf is now in charge of everything, while the newly desperate Peckem, destroyed by his own success, is roundly cursed ("Peckem, you son of a bitch . . . you stupid bastard!") by none other than the lowly Wintergreen (400).

Even Peckem's driving loyalty to the ethic of ambition has proved not as effective as the inherent lunacy of this universe. He has achieved all his ambitions, only to find himself at the mercy of a monomaniacal fool and a sneering punk. Scheisskopf can even be viewed as the god of the world of *Catch-22*, remote and ridiculous, wrapped up in arcane details of worthless purpose, insensitive to the humanity of those under his sway. He is the incompetent, little-minded yokel of Yossarian's earlier description, a description related—it should be recalled—to none other than Scheisskopf's wife.

Finally, it does not really matter who in this triumvirate runs the world of *Catch-22*, since all of them—Peckem, Scheisskopf, and Wintergreen—are reifiers of men and language. Whether their motives are personal power or parades, they turn human beings and words alike into mere things divorced from inherent meaning, the better to manipulate them.

VICTIMS AND VICTIMIZERS

As this section draws to a close, other elements of the hierarchy of victims and victimizers adjust themselves. In chapter 35, "Milo the Militant," Milo approaches Colonel Cathcart, who has just raised the missions to seventy, to ask for combat duty. Milo has gone about as far as he can go as a mess officer, having reached the point where he has raised his prices so high in the interests of profit that "all officers and enlisted men had to turn over all their pay to him in order to eat. Their alternative—and there was an alternative, of course, since Milo detested coercion and was a vocal champion of the freedom of choice—was to starve" (377). But someone higher up forces him to back down, despite a rigorous defense based on the law of supply and demand and "the historic right of free men to pay as much as they had to for the things they needed in order to survive" (377). Owing to his monomaniacal devotion to the profit motive, Milo is by this time more than ever on the side of the victimizers.

His plea to Colonel Cathcart takes his customarily sincere form: he insists that he wants to do his duty and fight "like the rest of the fellows" (378). Cathcart clearly respects Milo and couches his counterarguments carefully so as not to get a "black eye" in Milo's regard. He gives in only reluctantly and after much gentle opposition, which changes to glee when he realizes that Milo's powerful cartel must pass into his hands while Milo is on missions. Milo, with well-disguised guile for one originally so innocent, then manages to maneuver Cathcart, using the mind-bending complexity of his international enterprise, to order him to remain head of the cartel.

Furthermore, under Milo's persuasion Cathcart volunteers to have the men of the squadron fly missions in Milo's name, for which Milo gets the credit and the glory without the concomitant deaths, which will belong to the men alone. Milo also seeds Cathcart with the notion of raising the missions again and having Nately, who has finished his seventy and fears leaving his whore, volunteer for more. Milo even sells out his old friend Yossarian, after a brief demurrer. As Cathcart and Milo agree, "What's fair is fair" (384). Having defined fairness to their own satisfaction, Milo and Cathcart—prophets, respectively, of profit and personal ambition—are united. Milo has resolutely left the humble company of Yossarian's circle and joined the oppressors.

In fact, by the end of the novel all of the power-mongers end up on the same side: Milo makes Colonel Cathcart a vice president of his cartel, and Wintergreen's black market operation merges into M & M Enterprises. Given power of any kind in this world, one ends up inevitably on the side of the victimizers.

In Yossarian's immediate circle there are victims galore in this section of the novel. Death and injustice, helped along by the efforts of Milo, Cathcart, and Peckem, take a heavy toll in these chapters. Orr disappears in chapter 28; in chapter 30 McWatt kills Kid Sampson and then himself. Doc Daneeka is papered out of existence in the following chapter. Dunbar is "disappeared" at the end of chapter 34. Chief White Halfoat dies of pneumonia. After Milo and Cathcart have struck their deal, Dobbs and Nately collide on the very next mission and fall to their deaths. And though he manages to survive, it is near the end of this section, in chapter 36, that the chaplain is pronounced guilty of nonexistent crimes.

The chaplain's interrogation provides a déjà vu echo of Clevinger's; he, too, has been arrested on trivial charges and threatened by a pair of interrogators consisting of a colonel and a major. But true to the increasing darkening of the novel, this trial lacks the Marx Brothers dialogue of the first. It is not funny but sinister. The chaplain is trapped by his interrogators into one illogical corner after another; every positive statement he makes in his defense is turned against him, and Colonel Cathcart shows up just long enough to lie to the chaplain's disadvantage. Asking him about a tomato that Cathcart gave him, but which he has been accused of stealing, the interrogating colonel leads this exchange, based on a by now familiar syllogism:

> "Why did you steal it from Colonel Cathcart if you didn't want it?"
> "I didn't steal it from Colonel Cathcart!"
> "Then why are you so guilty, if you didn't steal it?"
> "I'm not guilty!"
> "Then why would we be questioning you if you weren't guilty?" (393)

Fact is of no importance to the interrogators, as one of them admits when, in response to the chaplain's protest that he is telling the truth, he rejoins, "I don't see how that matters one way or the other" (394).

Finally, the interrogating officers pronounce the chaplain guilty of all charges, "including crimes and infractions we don't even know about yet" (395). And then, to the chaplain's amazement, he is told to "take a walk." His punishment, if and when it comes, will be as arbitrary as his guilt, very much like the guilt and punishment of Kafka's protagonist in *The Trial*.

Even if Heller did not have *The Trial* in mind when he wrote *Catch-22*—and he maintains that it is Kafka in general rather than any one work that influenced him—this parallel is drawn quite clearly in Heller's later dramatization of the novel. In the play the chaplain's trial is virtually the climactic scene, underlining the stated theme of the play, which is, according to Heller's preface to the published version, "the unchecked misuses of authority in an atmosphere of war"; as such, it is dedicated to those put on trial by the Nixon administration during the Vietnam War, figures like Dr. Spock, the Berrigan

Brothers, Daniel Ellsberg, and the Chicago Seven.[83] More relevant to the novel's broader themes, however, is the chaplain's onstage comment in a letter to his wife: "Someone must have been telling lies about me, for without having done anything wrong . . ."[84] This is a direct paraphrase of the first line of Kafka's *Trial*: "Someone must have been telling lies about Joseph K., for without having done anything wrong he was arrested one fine morning."[85]

The last four chapters of this division, therefore, see Dunbar disappeared, Nately killed, and the chaplain persecuted, while Milo and Cathcart join forces and Peckem, Scheisskopf, and Wintergreen take charge. Thus the Kafkaesque bureaucracy of *Catch-22*, with its Orwellian manipulations of people and language, congeals; an idiotic god is in his reviewing stand, and all is wrong with the world for those like Yossarian and the chaplain who belong to the class of the manipulated. There matters stand as the final section of the novel begins.

By the time Scheisskopf takes command, Yossarian has reached a turning point. To continue to obey orders, even reluctantly, as he has done so far, is to condemn himself as well to personal extinction. And thus, as the last section of the novel begins at chapter 38, Yossarian finally overtly rebels.

9

Snowden, Orr, Sweden

"Yossarian marched backward," begins chapter 38, in a telling rhetorical bridge from the previous chapter, which ends with Scheisskopf's command that everybody should march. Yossarian, attuned to his very different drummer all along, has finally found the courage to march to it, in the opposite direction from everyone else "to make certain no one was sneaking up on him from behind" (401). This would be the behavior of a paranoid madman if he were not in fact correct; he is in danger of being killed if he continues to fly, or perhaps of being disappeared like Dunbar if *they* catch him. This final act of cowardice, oxymoronically, takes more courage than he or any one of his colleagues has shown so far. It is a courage born in part of desperation; all hope that he could outwait and outlive Cathcart's raising of the missions vanished with Nately's death. Yossarian is almost the only one left from his original group of peers, and only a peerless act might keep him from similar death, disappearance, or obliteration of self. He must at last take full responsibility for his own survival.

Responsibility rises to the fore as an important issue in these last chapters, beginning with this one, entitled "Kid Sister." The apparently disparate events of the chapter, mostly revolving around (like Yossarian, with the gun on his hip) his struggles with Nately's whore and the secret support of the other men for his revolt, are all connected by the question of responsibility. On the positive side, Yossarian's new position as a moral center for the other characters earns him a surprising amount of respect from the other men, as he learns when one after another "pops out" of the bushes. Even the gung ho combat fliers Appleby and Havermeyer, the antitheses to Yossarian in the squadron, turn up to urge him on, and Havermeyer suggests that if Yossarian's rebellion works, he might do the same. Yossarian's revolt, therefore, puts him in the role of heroic antihero, of potential savior or martyr. By taking full responsibility for his own life, he has taken to some extent the responsibility for the lives of the others.

But there is a negative side to being the responsible one, as Yossarian discovers when he delivers the news of Nately's death to Nately's whore. She holds Yossarian directly responsible for Nately's death and attempts to murder Yossarian in revenge. Indeed, she acts in the role of Fury, one of the Eumenides, throughout the rest of the novel, pursuing Yossarian with her implement of death in hand, seemingly unstoppable.

That Nately's whore holds Yossarian directly responsible for Nately's death seems just another of those mad injustices characteristic of the novel, until we reach chapter 39, "The Eternal City." It begins with Milo primly lecturing Yossarian on his duties as they fly to Rome, where Yossarian is going AWOL in order to take responsibility for Nately's whore's kid sister. The lecture ends with the observation that "Morale was deteriorating and it was all Yossarian's fault" (414).

Yossarian half acknowledges his fault in the next paragraph, when he comes to an understanding of why Nately's whore blames him:

Why the hell shouldn't she? It was a man's world, and she and everyone younger had every right to blame him and everyone older for every unnatural tragedy that befell them; just as she, even in her grief, was to blame for every man-made misery that landed on her kid sister and on all other children behind her. Someone had to do something sometime. Every victim was a culprit, every culprit a victim, and somebody had to stand up sometime to try to break the lousy chain of inherited habit that was imperiling them all. (414)

For the rest of this chapter, Rome—The Eternal City—becomes the world, and Yossarian an Everyman confronting the miseries and injustices the world offers up and wrestling with his own responsibility for them.

THE INFERNAL CITY

There have been suggestions, even before Yossarian's journey to the end of night, that he has had some responsibility for the events thus far. When Milo says "it was all Yossarian's fault," he echoes a phrase used much earlier at the beginning of the previous section: "In a way it was all Yossarian's fault, for if he had not moved the bomb line during the Big Siege of Bologna, Major ——— de Coverley might still be around to save him, and if he had not stocked the enlisted men's apartment with girls who had no other place to live, Nately might never have fallen in love with his whore . . ." (294).

In the context of the narration, *it* is not made specifically clear—that is, the "it" in "it was all Yossarian's fault"; this is another of those sentences with misjoined clauses which are used for rhetorical effect throughout the text. As critic Stephen L. Sniderman notes, the "he" in the second half of the sentence looks at first as though it refers to Yossarian, though it must refer to Major ——— de Coverley.[86] This sentence links, at least grammatically, Nately's whore and Yossarian's fault.

The same critic blames Yossarian directly or indirectly for a surprising number of the novel's episodes and even deaths. Sniderman finds him responsible for Dobbs not murdering Cathcart, for Nately's broken nose, for the CID investigations of Major Major and Chaplain Tappman that resulted from his playful censoring of letters, for the inception of Milo's cartel, which begins with the dried fruit Yossarian is receiving for his nonexistent liver condition, for the deaths of Kraft and his crew over Ferrara when Yossarian goes over the target a second time, for Daneeka's presence on McWatt's flight register and thus for the bureaucratic death of Daneeka, and more tenuously for many other such incidents.[87] Colonel Cathcart, it will be recalled, also found Yossarian responsible for many of his "black eyes."

But even where the chain of events does not lead directly back to Yossarian, he is guilty of one common crime through most of the novel, the crime of complicity. Up to this point, like all of his colleagues, Yossarian has let the likes of Cathcart, Korn, and Milo more or less have their way, offering little more than complaints and token resistance, followed by reluctant compliance. When the temptation for a genuine moral stance comes up, as during the briefing before the bombing of the Italian village, Yossarian, like Dunbar, is quickly silenced by Korn's cynical appeal to survival anxieties: here as at so many other places, Yossarian adopts the Old Man's ethic of survival, regardless of moral consequences, and at best he and Dunbar assuage their consciences with subterfuge.

Though he has already rebelled and further defied military protocol by heading on his quest through Rome without official permission, Yossarian's night journey in "The Eternal City" marks his turning point as moral man. It begins with his visit to the brothel in search of Nately's whore and her kid sister; the brothel, however, has been vandalized by MPs and carabinieri, and the women have been chased out into the street. Even the Old Man has died, evidence that the ethic of survival has its limitations. The only one who remains is the old woman who kept the place in order. She informs Yossarian that the MPs offered "Catch-22" as their rationale for committing this act. Over the course of the novel, the range of Catch-22 has expanded in scope, from the catch that prevents a crazy airman from being grounded, to the rule that dictates one must always obey one's commanding officer, to the catch-all offered by the old woman: "they have a right to do anything we can't stop them from doing" (416).

This ultimate Catch-22 disguises as morality—"right"—a rule of brute force. The whole intent of ethical codes is to provide rules for restraining the violent propensities of the human animal, but here is a rule that gives permission for that very abuse. The powerful are not only fully capable of victimizing the weak, they have the self-defined *right* to do so.

For once, Yossarian demonstrates he is not fooled by the spurious existence of the Catch: "Catch-22 did not exist, he was positive of that, but it made no difference. What did matter was that everyone thought it existed, and that was much worse . . ." (418). Catch-22 is thus not objective fact, but—once more—a formulation of mere words, a pseudoreality defined by those in power and taken on faith by everyone, with the definition eternally metamorphosing to suit the needs of power. True to the nature of this world, therefore, it stands as a governing fiction, more important and powerful than any of the facts it displaces. Like all use of language in the novel, the overarching construct of Catch-22 "controls rather than depicts, creates rather than recreates, predetermines rather than presupposes reality."[88]

The rest of the chapter demonstrates this rule of unchecked force in operation. Yossarian seeks out Milo to take advantage of the latter's considerable power in helping him find the whore's little sister, and Milo shows the moral willingness to assist until a whiff of tobacco smuggling sends him hypnotically after the black market, a slave to his lust for profit. Yossarian, left helpless, wanders the surreal streets of the ruined Eternal City, witnessing the eternal injustices of human life in a cosmos that does not care.

The scenes of pain, cruelty, and misery that parade "almost on cue" before Yossarian that night seem a sordid blend of *Esquire* naturalism and the grotesque absurdities of West, Céline, and Kafka. Heller has cited Dostoyevski's *Notes from the Underground* as a model for the chapter, as well as *Crime and Punishment*,[89] and that novel's antihero Raskolnikov receives passing mention in the narrative; both of these works delineate Dostoyevski's gloomy attitude toward the pervasive evil in the human soul and the necessity for individual moral responsibility.

In page-long paragraphs the narrative describes a sequence of tableaux, many of them paired with characteristic déjà vu: a poverty-stricken child and a poverty-stricken mother, a drunken soldier pressing himself upon a drunken woman, a man beating a dog and a man beating a boy, a soldier in convulsions and another with a bleeding, toothless mouth, and everywhere crass, insensitive policemen and other figures of authority ruling as "mobs with clubs" (426). Yossarian guiltily flees all these scenes of misery and injustice. Like the occasional groups of onlookers, he does not have sufficient moral courage to intervene. His sense of guilt comes to a head when he passes an old woman fruitlessly pursuing a younger woman. He tells himself that he will help if only the older woman asks him to or cries out. But before she can notice him or follow him, he hurries away "in shame because he had done nothing to assist her. He darted furtive, guilty glances back as he fled in defeat . . ." (426).

Minna Doskow has suggested Yossarian's night journey is a walk through a Dantesque, though man-made hell, in which neither Yossarian nor anyone can gain hope or redemption.[90] With its sinister and violent authority figures it typifies in concentrated form the morally inverted world of *Catch-22*, in which every victim is a culprit by dint of not fighting back and thus implicitly accepting the authority imposed from above. As in Kafka, the victim *can* be guilty.

The climax of this chapter comes when Yossarian reaches the officers' apartment and discovers that Aarfy has raped the maid and pushed her out the window to her death. Aarfy is one of those many characters who consistently looks worse as the novel progresses, though, as David H. Richter observes, "his character is not so much altered as progressively revealed" through the repetitive structure of the narrative[91]; he himself does not change but, as layer of meaning succeeds layer, our understanding of him changes. Each time he appears in a major scene his insensitivity becomes more brutish and horrifying. In an earlier and lighter moment Aarfy had threatened to shove a woman out the window, as had the group of naked generals in the previous section. But when he actually makes good on the threat, the act brings an entirely new and sinister significance to Aarfy and to his genial, oft-repeated insistence that he never has to pay for a woman.

When Yossarian, horrified, confronts Aarfy with the enormity of what he has done, we see in his wide-eyed confusion what Hanna Arendt called, in reference to the Nazis, "the banality of evil." Aarfy is another of those morally insane characters, like Milo and Cathcart, who cannot understand right and wrong in any traditional sense. Aarfy simply raped the maid because she had no significance to him as a human being and threw her out the window for the same reason, since he "couldn't very well let her go around saying bad things about us" (427). Yossarian takes the stance of moral arbiter here and manages to prick Aarfy's conscience enough to make him uncomfortable. But when the MPs show up as if to justify Yossarian by arresting Aarfy, they instead arrest Yossarian for being AWOL. Not surprisingly, given our understanding of this world, an exercise of unjust force leading to murder is no crime; defying the paper regulations of the military bureaucracy is.

Having survived his antiheroic quest through the underworld, Yossarian, like more traditional heroes, returns to society an outcast, ready to face his most severe moral trial.

THE ETERNAL CATCH

At the end of Yossarian's journey from The Eternal City back to Pianosa, surrounded by an orderly mob of MPs with clubs, he receives a surprise: he is to be sent home. His revolt has apparently succeeded.

There is, of course, a catch. In order to return to the States without penalty, Yossarian must become "one of the boys." He must ally himself with Cathcart and Korn so that they do not look bad with higher-ups like Scheisskopf and Peckem, and so that the other men will go on flying missions without rebelling. In short, Yossarian will win his battle for survival only by compromising with those in power and thus giving up his moral principles.

In this scene, Yossarian plays Christ to the temptations of Korn's cynical and amoral Satan. Indeed, like Dostoyevski's Christ in "The Grand Inquisitor," Yossarian, according to Korn, has made the men unhappy by showing them they have a choice. By his own admission Korn is "an intelligent person with no moral character at all" who is thus in an ideal position to appreciate Yossarian as "an intelligent person of great moral character who has taken a very courageous stand" (432). With typical cynicism Korn appeals to Yossarian's survival anxieties; if Yossarian does not accept the "odious" deal, he either goes back into combat or to court-martial, with the certainty of a long, unpleasant punishment. If he trades in his soul, on the other hand, he gains the world.

Since Cathcart and Korn, guardians of the ethic of ambition, have represented the main target of Yossarian's outrage throughout the novel, and since Korn's deal would require betraying his principles, his newly heightened moral consciousness, and the men who had supported his revolt, Yossarian balks at accepting it. But he finds a way through the use of the same kind of self-justifying logic used by Cathcart and Milo at other points:

> "But what the hell!" Yossarian exclaimed. "If they don't want to fly more missions, let them stand up and do something about it the way I did. Right?"
> "Of course," said Colonel Korn.
> "There's no reason I have to risk my life for them, is there?"
> "Of course not." (438)

With this single lapse, Yossarian opts to join the morally insane system he has fought for so long. But his lapse does not last long. His conscience returns to prick him in a very real and literal sense, in the form of Nately's furious whore and her knife. Almost supernaturally she reappears as he walks out of the embrace of Cathcart and Korn and stabs him, as if in revenge for his newest and worst crime of complicity.

Yossarian wakes in the hospital and in delirium experiences a host of sinister visitations, from dangerously ineffectual doctors and clerks, to Aarfy and Korn, to malicious interrogators and a diabolical figure who says only "We got your pal, buddy. We got your pal,"—a figure whom Minna Doskow literally takes to be the Devil.[92] He briefly wakes to a short conversation with his good angel, the chaplain, and remains conscious long enough to renounce his deal with Korn. He seems to be right back where he started in the first hospital visit of the novel, with no choice but to fly more missions or find subtle means of avoiding them. This is a sadder, wiser Yossarian than the flippant cynic of the first chapters, however. He recognizes that *they*—the powerful forces of death and injustice, human and cosmic—do have all his pals, even, it turns out, Hungry Joe, who has died in his sleep under Huple's cat. His only surviving friend is the chaplain, who lives under constant threat of punishment.

The moral stance Yossarian takes in this scene is wholly at odds with the pure survival ethic of the earlier Yossarian. Yossarian chooses to return to combat rather than betray the men by accepting Korn's odious deal. This is certainly not the sort of ethic Nately's Old Man implied when he told Nately to ask Yossarian and Dunbar for confirmation of his own cynical survivalism. The Old Man's ethic would dictate that Yossarian accept the deal and save himself. But for this Yossarian, unlike the Old Man, there is now an ethical principle higher than that of mere survival at any cost.

The quandary Yossarian finds himself in is brought to a head by the climactic scene of this chapter—chapter 41, "Snowden"—which finally details in full the death of the young airman Yossarian treated in the skies above Avignon. It is the last of several such teasing flashbacks, and the only time dislocation of this last section of the novel. Though Snowden's death occurred at the midpoint of the story, its full dramatic effect has been saved for last, where it not only caps the serious message of the novel, but also figures in the middle of Yossarian's rebirth as moral man. The ever-expanding and deepening significance of the event typifies the purpose of the cyclical nature of the narrative; the nonlinear, nonrational portrayal of this and other events is reminiscent of the torture machine in Kafka's "In the Penal Colony," where the name of one's crime is scratched into the flesh over and over until the message strikes, nonrationally, with a sudden burst of enlightenment. Our enlightenment comes with Yossarian's when we finally see Snowden "spill his secret," and Yossarian reads in his exposed entrails, in a grotesque parody of a traditional method of fortune-telling, one of nature's lessons—that "The spirit gone, man is garbage" (450).

The lesson is double-edged, however. It suggests that since man is matter, man is mortal, and that given matter's fragility life should be protected. This seems to be the belief Yossarian held inviolate during all of his hospital visits, from the hospital visit in the Bologna section of the novel when he ruminates on the thousand deaths he, as a coward, might suffer, all the way back to his first experience as a malingerer while still training in the States. The former could have been a consequence of his Snowden experience, but certainly not the latter, since it occurred before he had even entered combat.

On the other hand, the paragraph concerning the lesson of Snowden's secret also gives some priority to spirit. Man is garbage only when the spirit leaves. "Spirit" could mean the animate aspect of the body, related to its root meaning of "breath" and implied in the adjective "spirited," but it also possesses the sense of metaphysical soul, rooted in morality and transcendence. Without life, man is garbage, but without a soul man is garbage, too. Yossarian's paradox in this chapter, as he talks to the chaplain and recalls the entire Snowden episode, is that he cannot keep his spirit intact in both senses at once; either he returns to flying missions and loses his life, or he goes along with Korn and loses his soul. Either way he is garbage, mere matter. Unlike most of the earlier choiceless choices of the novel, this one has real meaning.

The dialogue over this problem takes up most of the last chapter, as Yossarian discusses it with Major Danby. Danby is one of those few characters in the novel—along with the chaplain and Major Major, Clevinger and Nately—who is victimized by his own adherence to traditional ideals. He is by background a liberal university professor who shares the chaplain's inability to stand up to authority and Clevinger's willingness to make excuses, on idealistic grounds, for the abuses of the powerful. In fact, while arguing with Danby Yossarian recognizes with a sense of déjà vu some of the exchanges he had with Clevinger in the novel's early chapters. Yossarian insists to Danby that he wants to fight for ideals like patriotism and "the dignity of man," but that everywhere he looks he finds Scheisskopfs, Peckems, Cathcarts and Korns "cashing in on every decent human impulse and every human tragedy" (455). Danby's ineffective answer is to "try not to think of them" (454) and to fight only for the ideals, but Yossarian will neither be treated like "a sucker" nor be condemned to death merely for the ambitions of the stupid and vile who preside over him. But since the powerful are united against them—Milo, Cathcart, and Wintergreen are all in business together now, and the ambitious and amoral Aarfy is willing to bear false witness against Yossarian—Danby and Yossarian find themselves at a dead end; they agree "there is no hope" (458). In this mad and unjust universe no impulse rooted in rational thought or traditional morality will work.

It takes, therefore, a wholly rational irrationality, a courageous cowardice, the heroism of a fool, to reverse the very real hopelessness of Yossarian and his fellow survivors. No sooner have Danby and Yossarian agreed that there is no hope for them than the chaplain enters bearing glad tidings: Orr has reappeared in Sweden. The chaplain ranks this resurrection from the dead a miracle and proclaims his renewed belief in God. For Yossarian the realization that Orr had long planned this journey to peace and freedom restores his faith in human potential and brings hope back by suggesting that there is an alternative to becoming just another Snowden or Mudd, another generic dying boy.

Before this news Yossarian had held Orr to be among the helpless victims of this world, "a happy and unsuspecting simpleton" who is just the sort to be lied to, cheated, bullied, and abused throughout his life (321). Yossarian thinks him a congenial, though practical imbecile who cannot look out for himself. By the time of his disappearance Orr had flown less than twenty missions and had been shot down on nearly every one—proof to Yossarian of Orr's desperate haplessness.

Now, with the news of Orr's intricately thought-out desertion, Orr becomes holy fool, a hero for those—like Yossarian and Danby and Chaplain Tappman—vying with an oppressive alliance of forces beyond their control. Orr has leaped beyond the system. He has defied probability and power, beating the system at its own game of chaining rational means to irrational goals; his planning of his escape has been as methodical as his rebuilding of the tent stove. Within the Catch-22 limitations of the world of the novel, Orr's success is indeed a miracle of human perseverance. Even his name suggests that he represents an alternative to the internally consistent illogic of the system; it is noteworthy that Orr is the only important character *not* to have a chapter named after him, as though he does not really belong in this world.

As a near miracle, Orr's clever desertion prompts the three victimized characters of this chapter to their own leaps of faith. Yossarian jumps to the decision to desert and head for Sweden himself; the chaplain makes up his mind to stand up to the abusers of power, and even Danby, after trying to dissuade them both, finally thrusts money into Yossarian's hands and urges him on his way. It is Danby who, after reminding Yossarian that his conscience will never let him rest, alerts him to the presence of Nately's furious whore, the embodiment of Yossarian's conscience, who waits to stab at him as he leaps into his uncertain future.

THE PROBLEM OF THE ENDING

The conclusion of the novel has proved controversial ever since its publication. For many who otherwise liked the book, the ending represents too much of a change in tone. The picaresque Yossarian, who has been whoring, lying, malingering, and dodging his official duties in the interest of self-preservation throughout the story, seems little related to the straightforwardly decent Yossarian of the last chapter, who sincerely and plaintively argues that he has done his patriotic part for the war effort, with almost none of the cynical snideness we have come to expect from him. The complaints from critics began with the earliest reviews. Norman Mailer, for instance, who greeted most of the novel with qualified praise, complained that the last five pages were "hysterical, sentimental and wall-eyed for Hollywood."[93] Vance Ramsey found the earlier Yossarian convincing, but "the last stage of his development not so convincing," and felt that the final four chapters have an unfortunate "discursive quality not found in most . . . of the novel."[94] Similar comments from others ranged from distress with Yossarian for deserting instead of standing firm to fight the war or the system, to distress with Heller for exchanging "the Fools' cap for the Preacher's robes."[95] Heller was thus castigated for not taking a moral stance and, on the other hand, for taking one.

There should be little doubt by now, given the ethical dialectic of the latter part of the book, that Heller's intent at the book's end was primarily moral. He has been clear on this issue in interviews, telling George Plimpton of the *Paris Review* that "*Catch-22* is concerned with physical survival against exterior forces or institutions that want to destroy life or moral self"[96] and elsewhere noting that the novel dramatizes "the birth of Yossarian's consciousness of himself as a moral being. Through most of *Catch-22* Yossarian feels all that he wants to do is survive the war. . . . In the hospital he finds that he can't accept [Korn's deal] because there's moral life inside him."[97]

A more difficult charge to answer is that made by Thomas Blues: that Heller changes the terms of the argument at the end. Instead of fleeing the war "because it is the only *humanely* possible action," Yossarian deserts only when he learns about Orr.[98] More damning, in Blues's view, is Yossarian's plaintive argument that he has been doing his patriotic duty for the war effort all along, which is a "violation of the structure, for the reader is quite aware that the historical World War II is of no importance in the novel except as a metaphor of a world in which order, truth, and humanity have been ruthlessly abolished. . . ."[99]

The best counterarguments anyone can offer to these and similar demurrers regarding the sudden change in tone, character, and direction at the book's close must appeal to the nontraditional nature of its form. Heller's book is not a novel in the strict sense of the word—rooted in mimesis, psychological realism, and linear development of character and plot—but an antinovel, parodying the novel's form even while undermining reader expectations, the way an antihero parodies and undermines the character of a conventional hero.

David H. Richter gives the best possible defense of *Catch-22*'s problematic ending by underlining its objective—which he discusses in terms of rhetorical "closure"—of trying to provide a concrete and prescriptive conclusion to his story, as opposed to the open-endedness characteristic of modernism or the Kafkaesque absurd. What, asks Richter, are the realistic alternatives to Yossarian's leap of faith? "Heller could have killed Yossarian off, or he could have had Yossarian mindlessly accept the colonel's deal, or he could have done neither, but at the same time given us the feeling somehow that, no matter what Yossarian did, he would never, never get outside the reach of *Catch-22*."[100] Any of these conclusions would have kept the book consistently absurdist in the Kafka-Céline-West tradition. But Heller's agenda required a more hopeful conclusion. In fact, the ending was determined before most of the rest of the book; it was not an afterthought but the goal that Heller had in mind pretty much from the beginning.[101] He wanted to leave his readers with a call to action, even if it was the negative action of refusing to accept those forces that would destroy life or moral self. The book works one of the postmodern veins—not the self-referentiality of metafiction, as Adam J. Sorkin notes,[102] but the moral pointedness of fabulism; like all the great satires that precede it, *Catch-22* has a specific point to make.

The book's ending also affects the question of whether *Catch-22* is merely "absurd" or genuinely "Absurd." As noted above, the universe of the novel matches that of the existentialists in being devoid of inherent and divinely inspired meaning, and for most of the novel Yossarian plays the part of a picaresque trickster-hero, lying and lusting in the wholehearted pursuit of life for its own sake. As noted in the Bologna section, Yossarian has resembled Camus's Absurd Man in resisting the withering of conscious self in the face of the meaninglessness of the cosmos and the abuses of arbitrary authority. He has held onto his free will, despite the blows delivered to it by the hierarchy of social and cosmic purveyors of death and injustice, and has refused the inducements of idealism and traditional heroism that Camus views as a withdrawal from intellectual honesty.

The final scene of the novel, however, changes philosophical direction somewhat, suggesting a rejection of total meaninglessness. The chaplain regains his faith in God, Yossarian his faith in humanity. Indeed, when Yossarian jumps away from the whore's knife and runs away—either to Rome or to Sweden—his act suggests Kierkegaard's leap of faith, which Camus sees as a retreat from the Absurd. On the other hand, Yossarian does not embrace some incomprehensible Kierkegaardian Absolute—though it appears that the chaplain does. No quest for a Kafkaesque Law motivates Yossarian's flight; his leap is strictly antinomian, rooted not in rational prescriptions and purpose, but in irrational faith alone.

In fact, there is doubt that Yossarian even believes in his stated goal of reaching the utopian Eden of Sweden. When Danby insists that it is virtually impossible for Yossarian to get there, Yossarian replies, "Hell, Danby, I know that. But at least I'll be trying" (462). Heller has underlined the fact that Yossarian is "not going to get there" and "knows that"; his is purely "an act of opposition and an act of protest."[103] This, in turn, suggests that it is not the genuine expectation of success that motivates Yossarian—the real goal of refuge from the war—but the mere fact of rebellion, of refusing to deal with the system, or let the system deal with him, on its own terms. As Gary W. Davis observes, Yossarian is choosing between fictions: the first fiction is defined by the bureaucracy of the war, which defines reality with the oppressive antimonies of Catch-22, and the second is his own personal fiction of Sweden, a symbol of peace and freedom. The significant fact in his choosing his own fiction is his rejection of the fiction that has dominated him up to this point. But Yossarian is fighting for the sake of fighting, not for the sake of success, and he is taking pleasure and strength from the fact of fighting back. In this sense, perhaps, his desertion is still an Absurd act. The faith that Orr gives him, therefore, is an existentialist faith in the power of individual free will.

It is, of course, fitting that an antinomian antinovel should have such an antihero for a moral focus. Vance Ramsey has suggested that Yossarian is a "picaresque saint," using R. W. B. Lewis's term for the modern hero who, though having characteristics of the amoral, asocial trickster of the picaresque tradition, is seeking his own private meaning regarding man's place in society and the universe.[104] Ramsey also observes that Yossarian is "the kind of character the term 'anti-hero' should have been reserved for," not the weak, ever-failing schlemiel of, say, Kafka, West, and the black humorists, but one "aggressively and even belligerently anti-heroic, and in his anti-heroism . . . a direct challenge to the values and ideals which the world claims to hold."[105] As Jim Castelli notes, Yossarian is likened throughout the book to mythical heroes from Superman to Achilles,[106] though he "values human life more than honor, duty, and glory, the values we are told are heroic."[107] His particular brand of heroism thus turns the traditional heroic values on their heads, as it must given the inverted ethic of this world.

Perhaps Helen Weinberg offers the most apt description of Heller's protagonist at the book's end when she lays out the characteristics of her "activist hero." The activist hero grows out of the Kafkaesque and the Absurd, but defies the absurdity of the universe by seeking "an authentic identity he has created for himself, a self that refuses to participate in the schemes of a maddeningly reasonable world's failures and successes. . . . What is relevant is his choice, his goal, his actions, his exploration of possibles beyond the givens and beyond the probable, and his putting himself, a particular, beyond the confines of the absurdist realities."[108]

Yossarian's antinomian choice, then, is for choice itself: free will bound only by a respect for life—his own life and others' lives—freedom from the inverted logic and inverted values of the life-destroying fiction defined by Catch-22.

CODA: THE CATCH GOES ON

Catch-22 is one of those rare books: a first novel that secured its author's reputation. Even rarer is the work of fiction that can add a brand new term to the language; not a week goes by without someone in the media or public life referring to something as a "Catch-22" situation. It was obviously a term whose time had come.

Amid all the literary and ethical discussions the book engenders, one must never overlook the book's fabulist intent, its clear-cut satire on contemporary American life, and its message of antinomian revolt well suited to the decade in which it appeared. Heller told *The Realist* that he had set out to create "a work of fiction—of literary art" that "would be as contemporary as possible"[109]—contemporary, that is, with the postwar cold war era. Later in the same interview he complains of the transfer of wartime ideology to peacetime, as happened in the United States in the wake of World War II: "when this wartime emergency ideology is transplanted to peacetime, then you have this kind of lag which leads not only to absurd situations, but to very tragic situations."[110]

Throughout the sixties early critics of Heller's antinovel were fond of lifting events from the real world—or from the fiction we held to be real—and putting them in the context of the book. Protherough quotes "the story of six American soldiers who allege that they were forced to create from thin air heroic acts of imaginary combats so that a general in Vietnam could receive the Silver Star and the Distinguished Flying Cross before he left his division for a new assignment."[111] Josh Greenfield repeats an anecdote reported by a *New York Times* reporter in Vietnam about an Army general who announced at a briefing that he was happy that Army casualties had caught up with those in the Marines; when incredulously asked if he really meant "happy," the general replied, "Well, the Army should be doing their job too."[112] Catch-22 reared its head in the frequent reports of Vietnamese villages that American troops burned to save and of people who were killed to protect them from the enemy.

Later, as the Vietnam War wound down in the seventies, students of *Catch-22* had the events of Watergate to keep them busy with comparisons. They had the spectacle of a Republican president who had approved a burglary of the Democratic party election headquarters more or less on the grounds that the other party was trying to overthrow his government, who believed (and continues to believe) that the president was exempt from obeying the laws of the land. We saw language tortured by White House spokesmen to explain away exposed lies as "inoperative statements."

The 1980s have provided no fewer examples of the sort of twisted logic and language characteristic of Heller's book. Under a regime peopled by profiteering Milos, publicity-conscious Peckems, red-baiting Captain Blacks, and a Scheisskopf nominally in charge, it has been an era of fiction over fact, of the inversion of values and reason, and of the redefining of words, and thus realities. Catsup is a "vegetable" for lunch programs aimed at the undernourished, missiles are "peace-keepers," CIA-supported terrorists in Nicaragua and Angola are "freedom fighters," Central American client states dominated by the military and right-wing death squads are "democracies," and presidential misstatements have, under the clarifications of "spin control," become "presidential facts."

The Iran-Contra hearings of 1987 produced the striking spectacle of American officials and ex-officials and ex-officio officials dealing arms to the Iranian government, long branded the chief monger of terrorism by the State Department, and then channeling funds in the name of democracy, albeit against the express will of Congress and the American majority, into the administration's undeclared war in Central America; of a Marine colonel who warmed America's heart by insisting he would stand on his head in the corner if the President asked him to, demonstrating a blind obedience to authority worthy of Nuremberg; of a retired Air Force general turned arms dealer who insisted he had committed no crimes in trading arms to terrorists because he was operating as an agent of the President, but that he should be allowed to keep his profits since he was a private citizen. It is hard to know whether to compare such a figure to Milo Minderbinder or to those relatives of Nately's described in the deleted chapter separately published as "Love, Dad": "several retired generals and admirals who were dedicating the remaining years of their lives to preserving the American Constitution by destroying it. . . ."[113] We have seen administrators put in charge of civil rights programs because they opposed civil rights and put in charge of environmental protection agencies because they opposed environmental protection; we have had an attorney general who spent his entire tenure running one step ahead of the law.

Heller predicted more than once in the seventies that *Catch-22* would decline somewhat in status as the war issue of the Vietnam era died away; he predicted, in fact, that his second novel, *Something Happened*, would last longer since it dealt with more familiar and universal issues. But he underestimated the durability of the cold war environment that spawned his first book.

We still live in the world of *Catch-22*.

Appendix:
A Chronology of *Catch-22*

DATE	YOSSARIAN	OTHERS
1942	In basic training at Lowery Field, Colorado. Discovers hospital.	Wintergreen demoted, digging ditches.
1943	Cadet training in Santa Ana. Spends Thanksgiving with Scheisskopf's wife.	Clevinger's trial
Early 1944 *25 missions*	Arrives in Pianosa with Appleby and Kraft. Splendid Atabrine Insurrection.	
30 missions	Y. has 23 missions.	Col. Nevers killed. Cathcart arrives, raises missions.
March: Ferrara	Y. goes over bridge twice. Promoted to captain.	Kraft killed. Milo appointed mess officer.
April *35 missions* **[May]**	Y. and Orr accompany Milo on business flight ("Milo the Mayor").	Milo forms international cartel and buys Egyptian cotton crop. Major Major appointed squadron commander. Capt. Black begins Loyalty Oath Crusade. Milo arranges Orvieto deal. Mudd's death.

DATE	YOSSARIAN	OTHERS
June 4: Allies enter Rome	Y. accompanies Nately to Rome.	Nately falls in love. Returning from Rome, Major ——— de Coverley ends Loyalty Oath Crusade.
Late June: Bologna	Y. moves bombline and poisons squadron, sabotages intercom. With 32 missions after Bologna, meets Luciana in Rome.	Major Major becomes recluse. Major ——— de Coverley goes to Florence and disappears.
40 missions	Y. returns from Rome to hospital.	
45 missions	Reaches 38 missions before entering hospital again.	Milo bombs squadron.
July: Avignon	Y. moans during briefing. Snowden killed. Y. naked in tree during funeral. Receives medal for Ferrara.	
August *50 missions*	Y. in hospital again. Has 44 missions. Meets chaplain (chapter 1).	Clevinger disappears inside cloud. Soldier in white.
Late August		Cathcart calls chaplain in to discuss the *Saturday Evening Post*.
September *55 missions*	At 44 and 48 missions, Y. goes to Daneeka, and at 51 to Major Major, but neither will ground him.	
60 missions	Y. wounded in thigh. Interviewed by Major Sanderson. Begins affair with Nurse Duckett.	

Appendix: A Chronology of Catch-22

DATE	YOSSARIAN	OTHERS
		Cathcart volunteers group for Bologna again. Orr vanishes.
	Y. and Dunbar don't want to bomb Italian village. Y. threatens McWatt.	
		McWatt kills Kid Sampson then flies into mountain. Daneeka's "death."
65 missions *70 missions*		
Mid-October	Y. helps Nately rescue his whore from generals.	Nately's whore falls in love with him.
November	On Thanksgiving Y. breaks Nately's nose. With Dunbar, visits Nately in hospital.	
		Soldier in white comes back. Dunbar goes crazy and is "disappeared."
	Y. finishes 70 missions.	
December *80 missions*		Milo arranges with Cathcart to have other men fly in his name. Nately volunteers for his 71st mission and dies. Peckem replaces Dreedle. Scheisskopf in charge. Chaplain's trial.
	Y. refuses to fly more missions. Goes AWOL in Rome ("The Eternal City"). Korn's deal. Stabbed by Nately's Whore. Decides to desert.	Aarfy kills maid. Orr reaches Sweden.

Notes

1. Sam Merrill, "*Playboy* Interview: Joseph Heller," *Playboy*, June 1975, 68.

2. Louis-Ferdinand Céline, *Journey to the End of the Night*, trans. John H. P. Marks (Boston: Little, Brown, 1934), 13.

3. Céline, *Journey*, 50.

4. Merrill, "*Playboy* Interview," 68.

5. Arthur Schlesinger, Jr., "The New Mood in Politics," *Esquire* (January 1960):58.

6. Tony Tanner, *City of Words: American Fiction 1950–1970* (New York: Harper & Row, 1971).

7. Schlesinger, "The New Mood," 60.

8. Merrill, "*Playboy* Interview," 61.

9. Nelson Algren, "The Catch," *The Nation*, 4 November 1961, 358.

10. Robert Brustein, "The Logic of Survival in a Lunatic World," *New Republic*, 13 November 1961, 11–13.

11. [Roger H. Smith], "A Review: *Catch-22*," *Daedalus* 92 (Winter 1963):155–65.

12. Frederick R. Karl, "Joseph Heller's *Catch-22*: Only Fools Walk in Darkness," *Contemporary American Novelists*, ed. Harry T. Moore (Carbondale: Southern Illinois University Press, 1965), 134–42.

13. Norman Podhoretz, "The Best Catch There Is," *Doings and Undoings* (New York: Farrar, Straus & Giroux, 1964), 228–35.

14. For instance, Ihab Hassan, "Laughter in the Dark: The New Voice in American Fiction," *American Scholar* 33 (Autumn 1964):636–39.

15. Joseph J. Waldmeir, "Joseph Heller: A Novelist of the Absurd," *Wisconsin Studies in Contemporary Literature* 5, no. 3 (1964):192–96.

16. Constance Denniston, "The American Romance-Parody: A Study of Purdy's *Malcolm* and Heller's *Catch-22*," *Emporia State Research Studies* 14, no. 2 (1965):42–64. G. G. McK. Henry, "Significant Corn: *Catch-22*," *The Critical Review* 9 (1966):133–44.

Notes

17. Sanford Pinsker, "Heller's *Catch-22*: The Protest of a *Puer Eternis*," *Critique* 7, no. 2 (1965):150–62. Vance Ramsey, "From Here to Absurdity: Heller's *Catch-22*," *Seven Contemporary Authors*, ed. Thomas B. Whitbread (Austin: University of Texas Press, 1968), 99–118.

18. Caroline Gordon and Jeanne Richardson, "Flies in Their Eyes? A Note on Joseph Heller's *Catch-22*," *Southern Review* 3 (1967):96–105. Brian Way, "Formal Experiment and Social Discontent: Joseph Heller's *Catch-22*," *Journal of American Studies* 2 (1968):253–70.

19. J. P. Stern, "War and the Comic Muse: *The Good Soldier Schweik* and *Catch-22*," *Comparative Literature* 20 (1968):193–216.

20. Jesse Ritter, "Fearful Comedy: *Catch-22* as Avatar of the Social Surrealist Novel"; Eric Solomon, "From Christ in Flanders to *Catch-22*: An Approach to War Fiction"; and Victor J. Milne, "Heller's 'Bologniad': A Theological Perspective on *Catch-22*," can all be found in *A 'Catch-22' Casebook*, ed. Frederick Kiley and Walter McDonald (New York: Crowell, 1973). Jess Ritter, "What Manner of Men Are These," *Critical Essays on "Catch-22,"* ed. James Nagel (Encino Calif.: Dickenson, 1974), 45–46. James Nagel, "*Catch-22* and Angry Humor: A Study in the Normative Values of Satire," *Studies in American Humor* 1 (1974):99–106.

21. John W. Hunt, "Comic Escape and Anti-Vision: Joseph Heller's *Catch-22*," *Adversity and Grace: Studies in Recent American Literature*, ed. Nathan A. Scott, Jr. (Chicago: University of Chicago Press, 1968), 91–98. Eugene McNamara, "The Absurd Style in Contemporary American Literature," *Humanities Association Bulletin* 19, no. 1 (1968):44–49. Hamlin Hill, "Black Humor: Its Cause and Cure," *Colorado Quarterly* 17 (Summer 1968):57–64. Max F. Schulz, "Pop, Op, and Black Humor: The Aesthetics of Anxiety," *College English* 30 (1 December 1968):230–41. Bruce Janoff, "Black Humor, Existentialism, and Absurdity: A Generic Confusion," *Arkansas Quarterly* 30 (1974):293–304.

22. Nelvin Vos, "The Angel, the Beast, and the Machine," *For God's Sake Laugh!* (Richmond, Va.: John Knox Press, 1967), 53–58. James E. Miller, Jr., *Quests Surd and Absurd: Essays in American Literature* (Chicago: University of Chicago Press, 1968), 24–25.

23. Minna Doskow, "The Night Journey in *Catch-22*," *Twentieth Century Literature* 12 (1967):186–93.

24. Milne's essay is cited above. Jim Castelli, "*Catch-22* and the New Hero," *Catholic World* 211 (July 1970):199–202. Wayne Charles Miller, *An Armed American: Its Face in Fiction* (New York: New York University Press, 1970), 205–43. Daniel Walden, "'Therefore Choose Life': A Jewish Interpretation of Heller's *Catch-22*," in Nagel, *Critical Essays on "Catch-22,"* (Boston: G. K. Hall, 1984), 57–63.

25. James L. McDonald, "'I See Everything Twice!' The Structure of Joseph Heller's *Catch-22*," *University Review* 34 (1968):175–80. James M. Mellard, "*Catch-22*: *Déjà vu* and the Labyrinth of Memory," *Bucknell Review*

16, no. 2 (1968):29–64. Jan Solomon, "The Structure of Joseph Heller's *Catch-22,*" *Critique* 9, no. 2 (1967):46–57.

26. Doug Gaukroger, "Time Structure in *Catch-22,*" *Critique* 12, no. 2 (1970):70–85.

27. Thomas Allen Nelson, "Theme and Structure in *Catch-22,*" *Renascence* 23 (1971):178. Howard J. Stark, "The Anatomy of *Catch-22,*" in Kiley, *Casebook.*

28. Clinton S. Burhans, Jr., "Spindrift and the Sea: Structural Patterns and Unifying Elements in *Catch-22,*" *Twentieth Century Literature* 19 (1973):239–50.

29. Robert Merrill, "The Structure and Meaning of *Catch-22,*" *Studies in American Fiction* 14 (Fall 1986):139–52.

30. [Paul Krassner], "An Impolite Interview With Joseph Heller," *The Realist* 39 (November 1962):18–31.

31. George Plimpton, "The Craft of Fiction: Joseph Heller," *Paris Review* 15 (Winter 1974):126–47. Richard B. Sale, "An Interview in New York with Joseph Heller," *Studies in the Novel* 4, no. 1 (Spring 1972):63–74. Sam Merrill, "*Playboy* Interview," 59–61, 64–66, 68, 70, 72–74, 76.

32. Robert M. Scotto, *Catch-22: A Critical Edition* (New York: Delta, 1973). Kiley, *Casebook.*

33. James Nagel, *Critical Essays on "Catch-22."*

34. Joseph Weixlmann, "A Bibliography of Joseph Heller's *Catch-22,*" *Bulletin of Bibliography* 31 (1974):32–37.

35. H. R. Swardson, "Sentimentality and the Academic Tradition," *College English* 37 (April 1976):747–66.

36. James Nagel, "Two Brief Manuscript Sketches: Heller's *Catch-22,*" *Modern Fiction Studies* 20 (1974):221–24, and "The *Catch-22* Note Cards," *Studies in the Novel* 8 (1976):394–405.

37. Carol Pearson, "*Catch-22* and the Debasement of Language," *CEA Critic* 38, no. 4 (1976):30–35. Gary W. Davis, "*Catch-22* and the Language of Discontinuity," *Novel* 12 (1978):66–77. Adam J. Sorkin, "From Papa to Yo-Yo: At War with All the Words in the World," *South Atlantic Bulletin* 44, no. 4 (1979):48–65. Fred M. Fetrow, "Joseph Heller's Use of Names in *Catch-22,*" *Studies in Contemporary Satire* 1, no. 2 (1975):28–38.

38. Jerome Klinkowitz, *The American 1960s: Imaginative Acts in a Decade of Change* (Ames: Iowa State University Press, 1980). Morris Dickstein, *Gates of Eden: American Culture in the Sixties* (New York: Basic Books, 1977), 113–17.

39. Leon F. Seltzer, "Milo's 'Culpable Innocence': Absurdity as Moral Insanity in Catch-22," *Papers on Language and Literature* 15 (1979):290–310.

40. Richard G. Stern, *New York Times Book Review,* 22 October 1961, 50. Whitney Balliet, *New Yorker,* 9 December 1961, 247.

41. Solomon, "Structure of Heller's *Catch-22*," reprinted in Kiley, *Casebook*, 122–32. In this discussion page references will be from the latter.

42. Solomon, "Structure of Heller's *Catch-22*," 123.

43. Doug Gaukroger, "Time Structure," reprinted in Kiley, *Casebook*, 132–44. In this discussion page references will be from the latter.

44. Clinton S. Burhans, Jr., "Spindrift and the Sea," reprinted in James Nagel, *Critical Essays on Joseph Heller* (Boston: G. K. Hall, 1984), 40–51. In this discussion page references will be from the latter.

45. Robert Merrill, *Joseph Heller* (Boston: Twayne, 1987), 36. Merrill's discussion of chronology here is substantially the same as that in his essay "The Structure and Meaning of *Catch-22*," 139–52.

46. Burhans, "Spindrift and the Sea," 48. Merrill, *Joseph Heller*, 36.

47. Gaukroger, "Time Structure," 144.

48. See, for instance, Heller's interview with Richard B. Sale, "An Interview in New York," 65.

49. James L. McDonald, "I See Everything Twice!," 104; reprinted in Kiley, *Casebook*, 102–108. In this discussion page references will be from the latter.

50. Sale, "An Interview in New York," 65.

51. Sale, "An Interview in New York," 66.

52. Stark, "The Anatomy of *Catch-22*," in Kiley, *Casebook*, 145.

53. Frederick R. Karl, "Only Fools Walk in Darkness," in Kiley, *Casebook*, 164.

54. Walter Blair and Hamlin Hill, *America's Humor* (New York: Oxford University Press, 1978), 435. Underlining Heller's relationship with mainstream comedy is his long friendship with fellow Coney Islander Mel Brooks.

55. Gary W. Davis, "The Language of Discontinuity," in Nagel, *Critical Essays on Joseph Heller*, 62–74.

56. Stark, "The Anatomy of *Catch-22*," in Kiley, *Casebook*, 150.

57. Way, "Formal Experiment," 265.

58. S. J. Perelman, "The Customer Is Always Wrong," *The Most of S. J. Perelman* (New York: Simon & Schuster, 1958), 225.

59. Ritter, "Fearful Comedy," in Kiley, *Casebook*, 182.

60. Max F. Schulz, *Black Humor Fiction of the Sixties* (Athens: Ohio University Press, 1973), 87.

61. Helen Weinberg, *The New Novel in America: The Kafkan Mode in Contemporary Fiction* (Ithaca, N.Y.: Cornell University Press, 1970), 9.

62. Weinberg, *The New Novel*, 9.

63. Jay Martin, *Nathanael West: The Art of His Life* (New York: Farrar, Straus & Giroux, 1970), 246.

64. Schulz, *Black Humor Fiction*, 6.

65. Robert Scholes, *The Fabulators* (New York: Oxford University Press, 1967), 60.

66. Schulz, *Black Humor Fiction*, 7.

67. Albert Camus, *The Myth of Sisyphus and Other Essays*, trans. Justin O'Brien (New York: Vintage, 1955), 29.

68. Camus, *Sisyphus*, 98ff.

69. Jean Kennard, "Joseph Heller: At War with Absurdity," in Kiley, *Casebook*, 255.

70. Weinberg, *The New Novel*, 11.

71. David Galloway, *The Absurd Hero in American Fiction*, 2d ed. (Austin: University of Texas, 1981), 16.

72. Schulz, *Black Humor Fiction*, 91.

73. Nelson Algren, *The Man with the Golden Arm* (Garden City, N.Y.: Doubleday, 1949), 205. In his *Realist* interview, Heller referred to this novel as an "unconscious influence" (Krassner, "An Impolite Interview"; reprinted in Kiley, *Casebook*, 273–93:277). Indeed, it remained so at least into his next novel *Something Happened*, which takes its title from the episode in Algren's book when the junkie protagonist Frankie gets involved in a traffic accident that leaves his wife Sophie crippled; the boy who announces the accident comes on the scene crying, "Something happened." In a later interview, Heller told this episode as though it had actually occurred, suggesting that the influence of Algren's novel remained subliminal.

74. See the discussion of Yossarian and Milo in Gary Lindberg, *The Confidence Man in American Literature* (New York: Oxford University Press, 1982).

75. Merrill, "*Playboy* Interview," 64.

76. Leon F. Seltzer, "Milo's 'Culpable Innocence'"; reprinted in Nagel, *Critical Essays on Joseph Heller*, 74–92.

77. Milne, "Heller's 'Bologniad,'" in Kiley, *Casebook*, 65.

78. Milne, "Heller's 'Bologniad,'" 65.

79. Plimpton, "The Craft of Fiction," 134.

80. James Nagel, "Yossarian, the Old Man, and the Ending of *Catch-22*," in *Critical Essays on Catch-22*, 164–74.

81. Nagel, "Note Cards," reprinted in Nagel, *Critical Essays on Joseph Heller*, 52.

82. Stark, "The Anatomy of *Catch-22*," in Kiley, *Casebook*, 154.

83. *Catch-22: A Dramatization* (New York: Delacorte, 1973), xiv.

84. *A Dramatization*, 173.

85. Franz Kafka, *The Trial*, trans. Willa and Edwin Muir (New York: Schocken, 1956), 1. Considering the bond between Chaplain Tappman and Joseph K., it merits mention here that the same actor, Anthony Perkins, played

both roles in film, respectively under the direction of Mike Nichols and Orson Welles.

86. Stephen L. Sniderman, "'It Was All Yossarian's Fault': Power and Responsibility in *Catch-22*," *Twentieth Century Literature* 19 (1973):251–58; reprinted in Nagel, *Critical Essays on Joseph Heller,* 33–39:36.

87. Sniderman, "Yossarian's Fault," 35–36.

88. Sorkin, "From Papa to Yo-Yo," 54–55.

89. Sale, "An Interview in New York," 74.

90. Minna Doskow, "The Night Journey," in Kiley, *Casebook*, 166–74.

91. David H. Richter, *Fable's End: Completeness and Closure in Rhetorical Fiction* (Chicago: University of Chicago Press, 1974), 147.

92. Doskow, "The Night Journey," 172.

93. Norman Mailer, "Some Children of the Goddess," *Contemporary American Novelists*, ed. Harry T. Moore (Carbondale: Southern Illinois University Press, 1964), 13–14.

94. Ramsey, "From Here to Absurdity," 235.

95. W. Scammell, "Letter in Reply to Mr. Wain," *The Critical Quarterly* 5 (Autumn 1963):274; in Kiley, *Casebook*, 50.

96. Plimpton, "The Craft of Fiction," 141.

97. Sale, "An Interview in New York," 73.

98. Thomas Blues, "The Moral Structure of *Catch-22*," *Studies in the Novel* 3 (Spring 1971):76.

99. Blues, "Moral Structure," 76–77.

100. Richter, *Fable's End,* 163.

101. Krassner, "An Impolite Interview," in Kiley, *Casebook*, 287.

102. Sorkin, "From Papa to Yo-Yo," 55–56.

103. Krassner, "An Impolite Interview," 289.

104. Ramsey, "From Here to Absurdity," 233.

105. Ramsey, "From Here to Absurdity," 225.

106. Jim Castelli, "The New Hero," in Kiley, *Casebook*, 178.

107. Castelli, "The New Hero," 176.

108. Weinberg, *The New Novel*, 12.

109. Krassner, "An Impolite Interview," 275.

110. Krassner, "An Impolite Interview," 288.

111. Protherough, 203.

112. Josh Greenfeld, "22 Was Funnier Than 14," in Kiley, *Casebook*, 250.

113. "Love, Dad," in Kiley, *Casebook*, 310.

Selected Bibliography

Primary Sources

Catch-22. New York: Simon & Schuster, 1961.

Catch-22: A Dramatization. New York: Delacorte, 1973.

"Catch-22 Revisited." *Holiday,* April 1967, 44–60. Reprinted in *A "Catch-22" Casebook,* edited by Frederick Kiley and Walter McDonald, 317–32.

"Clevinger's Trial." In *The Best Short Plays of 1976,* edited by Stanley Richards. Radnor Pa.: Chilton, 1977.

God Knows. New York: Knopf, 1984.

Good as Gold. New York: Simon & Schuster, 1979.

"Love, Dad." *Playboy,* December 1969, 181–82, 348. Reprinted in *A "Catch-22" Casebook,* ed. Kiley and McDonald, 309–16.

"A Missing Chapter of *Catch-22*" [About calisthenics instructor at Lowery Field and Yossarian's discovery of the hospital]. *Playboy,* December 1987, 144–46, 184, 186.

No Laughing Matter. With Speed Vogel. New York: Putnam, 1986.

"On Translating *Catch-22* Into a Movie." *A "Catch-22" Casebook,* ed. Kiley and McDonald, 346–62.

Something Happened. New York: Knopf, 1974.

We Bombed in New Haven. New York: Knopf, 1968.

Secondary Sources

Books

Kiley, Frederick, and Walter McDonald, eds. *A "Catch-22" Casebook.* New York: Crowell, 1973. The first and still the most wide-ranging collection of materials on the first decade of *Catch-22.* Includes several reviews, critical essays, a pair of interviews, informal articles on the book and the movie, and the *Mad* magazine parody of the movie. Referred to below as "Kiley."

Merrill, Robert. *Joseph Heller.* Boston: Twayne, 1987. Critical studies of all of Heller's novels and plays. The section on *Catch-22* discusses the novel's generic classification as well as the relationship of structure and meaning.

Nagel, James, ed. *Critical Essays on Catch-22.* Encino, Calif.: Dickenson, 1974. Contains reviews and critical essays, some reprinted, some original and available nowhere else. Few overlaps with Kiley. Referred to below as "Nagel 1974."

Nagel, James, ed. *Critical Essays on Joseph Heller.* Boston: G. K. Hall, 1984. Essays on all of Heller's major works, including some solicited just for this volume, with a useful introductory essay by Nagel on the history of Heller scholarship. Referred to below as "Nagel 1984."

Potts, Stephen W. *From Here to Absurdity: The Moral Battlefields of Joseph Heller.* San Bernardino Calif.: Borgo, 1982. A slender monograph that links Heller's work through *Good as Gold* using themes of mortality and morality.

Scotto, Robert, ed. *Catch-22: A Critical Edition.* New York: Delta, 1973. The full text of the novel along with a number of critical essays. Referred to below as "Scotto."

Articles and Chapters of Books

Blues, Thomas. "The Moral Structure of *Catch-22,*" *Studies in the Novel* 3 (Spring 1971):64–97. Reprinted in Nagel 1974 and Scotto. Focuses on the moral argument of the book, noting a change of strategy that mars its ending.

Burhans, Clinton S., Jr. "Spindrift and the Sea: Structural Patterns and Unifying Elements in *Catch-22.*" *Twentieth Century Literature* 19, no. 4 (1973):239–50. Reprinted in Nagel 1984. A discussion of plot chronology and patterns.

Davis, Gary W. "*Catch-22* and the Language of Discontinuity." *Novel* 12, no.

1 (1978):66–77. Reprinted in Nagel 1984. A Derridan look at the linguistic fictions of the novel.

Doskow, Minna. "The Night Journey in *Catch-22*." *Twentieth Century Literature* 12 (January 1967):186–93. Reprinted in Kiley, Nagel 1974, and Scotto. Still the best close reading of "The Eternal City," with particular attention to religious imagery.

Gaukroger, Doug. "Time Structure in *Catch-22*." *Studies in Modern Fiction* 12, no. 2 (1970):70–85. Reprinted in Kiley and Nagel 1974. The first mostly accurate unraveling of the plot, refuting Jan Solomon's earlier article.

Kennard, Jean. "Joseph Heller: At War with Absurdity." *Mosaic* 4, no. 3 (Spring 1971):75–87. Reprinted in Kiley and Scotto. Discussion of novel's links to existentialist thought and its comic and rhetorical techniques.

[Krassner, Paul.] "An Impolite Interview with Joseph Heller." *The Realist* 39 (November 1962):18–31. Reprinted in Kiley and Scotto. The first major interview of Heller, with much information on the initial reception of *Catch-22* and its themes and techniques.

McDonald, James L. "'I See Everything Twice!' The Structure of Joseph Heller's *Catch-22*." *University Review* 34 (Spring 1968):175–80. Reprinted in Kiley. The function of repetition in the novel.

Mellard, James M. "*Catch-22*: *Déjà Vu* and the Labyrinth of Memory." *Bucknell Review* 16 (May 1968):29–44. Reprinted in Kiley and Scotto. Déjà vu as a controlling principle of plot and theme.

Merrill, Sam. "*Playboy* Interview: Joseph Heller." *Playboy*, June 1975, 59–61, 64–66, 68, 70, 72–74, 76. A long interview covering the genesis of *Catch-22* and *Something Happened*, as well as Heller's interests, favorite writers, and politics.

Milne, Victor J. "Heller's 'Bologniad': A Theological Perspective on *Catch-22*." *Critique* 12, no. 2 (1970):50–69. Reprinted in Kiley. Examines the book as Christian "mock epic" dramatizing different values of characters.

Nagel, James. "The *Catch-22* Note Cards." *Studies in the Novel* 8 (1976):394–405. Reprinted in Nagel 1984. A look at some of Heller's notes for the novel currently in the Brandeis University library.

Nelson, Thomas Allen. "Theme and Structure in *Catch-22*." *Renascence* 23, no. 4 (Summer 1971):178–82. A study of plot cycles and the theme of responsibility.

Plimpton, George. "The Craft of Fiction: Joseph Heller." *Paris Review* 15 (Winter 1974):126–47. A long, useful interview with much about Heller's work habits and influences on *Catch-22* and *Something Happened*.

Ramsey, Vance. "From Here to Absurdity: Heller's *Catch-22*," in *Seven Contemporary Authors*, ed. Thomas B. Whitbread. Austin: University of Texas Press, 1968. Reprinted in Kiley. An early essay relating the issues of sanity, absurdity, and antiheroism.

Selected Bibliography

Richter, David H. "The Achievement of Shape in the Twentieth Century Fable: Joseph Heller's *Catch-22*," in *Fable's End: Completeness and Closure in Rhetorical Fiction.* Chicago: University of Chicago Press, 1974. An analysis of Heller's method as representing a modern breakthrough in fabulist literature.

Sale, Richard B. "An Interview in New York with Joseph Heller." *Studies in the Novel* 4, no. 1 (Spring 1972):63–74. Covers many literary topics: the technique of *Catch-22* and *Something Happened,* then in progress, the history of *We Bombed in New Haven,* and Heller's appraisal of a number of writers, most in the tradition of the absurd.

Seltzer, Leon F. "Milo's 'Culpable Innocence': Absurdity as Moral Insanity in *Catch-22.*" *Papers on Language and Literature* 15 (1979):290–310. Reprinted in Nagel 1984. Brings together the issues of absurdity, insanity, and morality.

Sniderman, Stephen L. "'It Was All Yossarian's Fault': Power and Responsibility in *Catch-22.*" *Twentieth Century Literature* 19 (1973):251–58. Reprinted in Nagel 1984. Focuses on Yossarian's responsibility.

Sorkin, Adam J. "From Papa to Yo-Yo: At War with All the Words in the World." *South Atlantic Bulletin* 44, no. 4 (1979):48–65. Compares Heller's distrust of language with Hemingway's modernism.

Stark, Howard J. "The Anatomy of *Catch-22*," in Kiley, 145–58. An analysis of the book's structure and absurd intent.

Way, Brian. "Formal Experiment and Social Discontent: Joseph Heller's *Catch-22.*" *Journal of American Studies* 21, no. 2 (October 1968):253–70. The book as a revolutionary blend of naturalism and absurdity in the tradition of radical social protest.

Bibliographies

Keegan, Brenda M. *Joseph Heller: A Reference Guide.* Boston: G. K. Hall, 1978. Lists and annotates all works on Heller to 1977; especially useful on interviews.

Scotto, Robert M. *Three Contemporary Novelists: An Annotated Bibliography of Works by and about John Hawkes, Joseph Heller, and Thomas Pynchon.* New York: Garland, 1977. Primary and secondary bibliographies, broken into several subcategories: reviews, interviews, critical anthologies, etc.

Weixlmann, Joseph. "A Bibliography of Joseph Heller's *Catch-22.*" *Bulletin of Bibliography* 31 (1974):32–37. Cites over two hundred essays on *Catch-22* from 1961 to 1973.

Index

Index

Index

Walden, Daniel, 12
Waldmeir, Joseph J., 11
Way, Brian, 11, 43
We Bombed in New Haven, 8, 12
Weinberg, Helen, 60, 65, 114
Weixlmann, Joseph, 14

West, Nathanael, 3, 9, 65; *A Cool Million*, 62; *Miss Lonelyhearts*, 61–62
Whyte, W. H.: *The Organization Man*, 5, 73
Wilson, Charles E., 3, 78
Wintergreen, as reifier, 93–94

About the Author

Stephen W. Potts did his graduate work at the University of California at Berkeley on a Danforth Fellowship. After completing a dissertation on the magazine career of F. Scott Fitzgerald, he received a Ph.D. in English in 1980 and spent the next year as a Fulbright Lecturer in American literature at the Bayerische Julius-Maximilians Universität in Würzburg, West Germany. He has published short fiction as well as articles and monographs on Fitzgerald, Joseph Heller, and a number of American, British, and Slavic science fiction writers. As a visiting lecturer at the University of California at San Diego, he teaches popular literature and creative writing. He is currently marketing one novel and finishing another.